THE GOD OF THE BIBLE AND THE GOD OF THE PHILOSOPHERS

The Aquinas Lecture, 2016

THE GOD OF THE BIBLE AND THE GOD OF THE PHILOSOPHERS

by

Eleonore Stump

Under the auspices of the
Wisconsin-Alpha Chapter of Phi Sigma Tau

MARQUETTE
UNIVERSITY
PRESS

Under the auspices of the
Wisconsin-Alpha Chapter of Phi Sigma Tau

LIBRARY OF CONGRESS CATALOGING-IN-PUBLICATION DATA

Names: Stump, Eleonore, 1947- author.
Title: The God of the Bible and the God of the philosophers
    / by Eleonore Stump.
Description: first [edition]. | Milwaukee, Wisconsin:
    Marquette University Press, 2016. | Series: The
    Aquinas lecture; No.80, 2016 | Includes bibliographical
    references.
Identifiers: LCCN 2015045956| ISBN 9780874621891
    (hardcover: alk. paper) | ISBN 0874621895 (hardcover:
    alk. paper)
Subjects: LCSH: God—Biblical teaching. | Thomas,
    Aquinas, Saint, 1225?-1274. | God.
Classification: LCC BS544 .S78 2016 | DDC 211—dc23
LC record available at http://lccn.loc.gov/2015045956

♾ The paper used in this publication meets the minimum requirements of the American
National Standard for Information Sciences–
Permanence of Paper for Printed Library Materials, ANSI Z39.48-1992.

Association of American
University Presses

MARQUETTE UNIVERSITY PRESS
MILWAUKEE

The Association of Jesuit University Presses

The Philosophy Department of Marquette University on behalf of Phi Sigma Tau, the Philosophy Honors Society, each year invites a scholar to deliver a lecture in honor of St. Thomas Aquinas.

Dr. Eleonore Stump

The 2016 Aquinas Lecture, *The God of the Bible and the God of the Philosophers*, was delivered on Sunday, February 28, 2016, by Eleonore Stump,

Robert J. Henle Professor of Philosophy, Saint Louis University.

Prof. Stump has a B.A. in Classical Languages from Grinnell College, where she was valedictorian (1969). She also holds an M.A. in New Testament Studies from Harvard University (1971) and an M.A. and Ph.D. in Medieval Studies from Cornell University (1975). Before moving to Saint Louis University in 1992 to take up the Robert J. Henle Chair in Philosophy, she taught at Oberlin College, Virginia Tech, and Notre Dame. She has also had visiting appointments at the Wolfgang Goethe University (Frankfurt), Calvin College, Oxford (Oriel), Baylor University, the Pontifical Gregorian University, Aberdeen University, Princeton University, Wuhan University, and the Australian Catholic University. Among the distinguished lectures she has given are the Gifford lectures (Aberdeen), the Wilde lectures (Oxford), and the Stewart lectures (Princeton). Her numerous awards include the Robert Foster Cherry Award for Great Teaching (Baylor University, 2004), an honorary doctorate from Marquette University (2006), and the Aquinas medal (the American Catholic Philosophical Association, 2013). In 2012, she was inducted into the American Academy of Arts and Sciences. In 2014-15, with her colleague John Greco, she was awarded a $3.3 million Templeton grant for work on the topic "Intellectual Humility". She has been president of the Society of Christian Philosophers ((1995-98), the American

Catholic Philosophical Association (1999-2000), the American Philosophical Association, Central Division (2005-2006), and Philosophers in Jesuit Education (2013-2015). Prof. Stump has published extensively in metaphysics, philosophy of religion, and medieval philosophy, and her work has been translated into Polish, Russian, Chinese, Swedish, Italian, German, Spanish, and French. Among her books are her magisterial *Aquinas* (2003) and her extensive discussion of the problem of suffering *Wandering in Darkness* (2010). She has published more than 100 articles on topics as diverse as "Dialectic in the Eleventh and Twelfth Centuries: Garlandus Compotista", "Theology and Physics in *De Sacramento Altaris*: Ockham's Theory of Indivisibles", "Dante's Hell, Aquinas's Theory of Morality, and the Love of God", "Non-Cartesian Substance Dualism and Materialism without Reductionism", "Libertarian Freedom and the Principle of Alternative Possibilities", "Saadia Gaon on the Problem of Evil", "Augustine on Free Will," and "Love, By All Accounts".

To Prof. Stump's distinguished list of publications, the Philosophy Department and Phi Sigma Tau are pleased to add: *The God of the Bible and the God of the Philosophers*.

*For the great Dominican community,
for which I am so grateful*

"Looking on His Son with the Love
which each eternally breathes out upon the other,
the primal, indescribable Power created
all that spins through mind and space
with such harmony
that anyone who gazes on it
will surely savor Him."

(The opening of the canto introducing the Dominican
Doctors of the Church, Dante, *Paradiso*, Canto X, ll. 1-6;
trans. Eleonore Stump and Paul Philibert)

THE GOD OF THE BIBLE AND THE GOD OF THE PHILOSOPHERS

by

Eleonore Stump

Introduction

It is common among contemporary theologians and philosophers to suppose that the God of the Bible is radically different from the God of the philosophers. The God of the philosophers is generally understood to be the God of classical theism, whose standard divine attributes are those paradigmatically given by the great medieval philosophers of the three monotheisms, Averroes, Maimonides, and Aquinas. Some of the current trend towards open theism among philosophers of religion has its source in the twinned convictions that there is an inconsistency between the description of God given by the Bible and the characterization of God upheld by classical theism, and that the biblical portrayal is greatly preferable to the account of God accepted by classical theism.

To see the apparent inconsistency, take first the presentation of God in the Hebrew Bible; and consider, for example, the Bible's story of Jonah in the biblical book that bears his name.[1]

As that story opens, God comes to talk to Jonah, who knows God and recognizes God's voice right away. God tells Jonah to go to Ninevah and warn the people that their city will be destroyed in 40 days.

Jonah not only understands what God is saying to him, but he understands that it is God who is saying it. Only Jonah does not want to do what God is asking of him, and so he reacts to God's speech by taking ship to a far country. Once Jonah is on board ship, God responds to Jonah's attempt to run away by making a violent storm that imperils everyone on the ship. When the sailors cast lots to see whose fault it is that there is a storm, God somehow brings it about that the lots come out to indicate Jonah. And when, at Jonah's urging, the sailors throw Jonah overboard in consequence, God responds to their action by calming the sea for them.

Cast overboard, Jonah begins to drown; and, as he goes down in the water, he prays to God for help. In response, God prepares a rescue for Jonah in the form of a large sea beast who saves Jonah by swallow-

---

1   It should be said in this connection that some thinkers take the book of Jonah as intended to be read allegorically or in some other analogical way. For my purposes, taking the story literally is appropriate since it is the picture of God in the literal story that is opposed to the picture of God apparently given by classical theism.

ing him whole. Inside the beast, Jonah finally prays to God a prayer accepting the task that God originally set him. Because of this prayer of Jonah's, God speaks to the beast, who hears and obeys God's voice and spits Jonah out on shore. Then Jonah does in fact go to the people of Ninevah to give them God's message that their city will be destroyed in 40 days.

The result of Jonah's prophesying God's plan for the city's imminent destruction is that the whole Ninevite people repent in dust and ashes. Because they do, God responds to their repentance by abrogating the destruction of the city which he had told Jonah to announce.

And this is not yet the end of the story. When Jonah is filled with anger at God's failure to follow through on the message of destruction that God told Jonah to announce to Ninevah, God teaches Jonah a lesson about mercy. He makes a fast-growing plant appear by Jonah and then quickly die. When Jonah laments the death of the plant, then in interactive conversation with Jonah God uses the example of the plant to try to get Jonah to understand God's actions towards Ninevah.

In this story, the God of the Hebrew Bible is so present to human beings that they know God and relate to God in highly personal ways. For his part, God converses with people, responds to their needs and prayers, apparently changes his mind about what he has told them, issues prophecies about them that he seems to decide not to fulfill, and in general engages with individual human persons in close and personal ways.

One might say that the God portrayed in this story and in the Hebrew Bible generally is very human. When Genesis says that human beings are made in the image of God, the stories of God in the Hebrew Bible bear out the claim. As the story of Jonah illustrates, the humanity of human persons has its correlative image in the responsive and personally present God of the Hebrew Bible. There is a rich anthropomorphism here that the stories underscore and approve.

Something analogous can be said about the representation of God in the New Testament. Given the nature of the New Testament and its focus on Christ, the case for this claim has to be made on the basis of a relation between Christ and God. So, consider, for example, the way in which, in his commentary on the Gospel of John, Aquinas sees Christ and Christ's relation to God. Although Aquinas is generally considered one of the main proponents of classical theism, the God he presents in his remarks about Christ in his commentary on John is also very human, one might say.

To begin with, at various places in his commentary, Aquinas makes it clear that, in his view, Christ can be known in personal relationship even by people living after Christ's earthly ministry. Speaking to his own readers, Aquinas says, "If then you ask which way to go, accept Christ, for he is the way.….

If you ask where to go, cling to Christ, for he is the truth, which we desire to reach…. If you ask where to remain, remain in Christ because he is the life."[2]

That these descriptions of connection between human beings and Christ are not meant as metaphors for the acceptance of theological truths but are meant to be taken literally, as descriptions of personal relationship to Christ and personal knowledge of Christ, is attested by myriad texts in this same commentary. Consider, for example, this comment of Aquinas's on Christ's claim that he is the true vine: "Christ is a true vine producing a wine which interiorly intoxicates us… and which strengthens us. … [T]hose united to Christ are the branches of this vine."[3]

Without personal relationship to Christ and personal knowledge of Christ, one could hardly be said to be *united* with Christ.

---

2   *Commentary on the Gospel of John*, Chapter 14, lecture 2. I like and therefore have used the translations from *Commentary on the Gospel of John, Chapters 13-21 by St. Thomas Aquinas*, trans. Fabian Larcher and James A. Weisheipl (Washington: Catholic University of America Press, 2010), but I have felt free to modify those translations in the few places where I felt I could do better. Page numbers in references to this work are to the Larcher and Weisheipl translation. This quotation occurs on p. 55-6 of their translation.

3   *Commentary on the Gospel of John*, Chapter 15, lecture 1, p. 96-8.

It is important to understand in this connection that Aquinas takes a person's knowledge of Christ and relationship to Christ to be that person's knowledge of God and relationship to God as well. For example, in commenting on Christ's rebuke to Philip that anyone who has seen Christ has seen the Father, Aquinas remarks,

> [Christ] shows that knowledge of the Son is also knowledge of the Father, [and] he ... [asserts] the disciples' knowledge of the Father. ... [T]here is no better way to know something than through its word or image, and the Son is the Word of the Father. ... Therefore, the Father is known in the Son as in his Word and proper image.[4]

And Aquinas goes on to say, "[The Father] was in the incarnate Word because they had one and the same nature, and the Father was seen in the incarnate Christ."[5]

On Aquinas's view, that relation between Christ and God is also the reason why Christ disapproved of Philip's request that Christ show the disciples the Father. Aquinas says, "[Christ] is displeased with ... [Philip's] request because the Father is seen in the Son."[6]

---

4   *Commentary on the Gospel of John*, Chapter 14, lecture 2, p. 58.

5   *Commentary on the Gospel of John*, Chapter 14, lecture 2, p. 59-60.

6   *Commentary on the Gospel of John*, Chapter 14, lecture 3, p. 63.

In fact, not only is God the Father known in Christ, but, on Aquinas's views, part of the divine purpose in the incarnation is precisely to make God known. God wants human beings in this life to know him, and that is why God provides an incarnation. Aquinas says, "[N]o one can acquire a knowledge of the Father except by his Word, which is his Son... [S] o God, wanting to be known by us, takes his Word, conceived from eternity, and clothes it with flesh in time."[7]

As far as that goes, on Aquinas's views, this knowledge of God is necessary for being in grace, that is, for being in an at least minimally morally acceptable condition.[8] In commenting on the passage in which Christ says that those who persecute his followers will do so because they lack knowledge of God, Aquinas says of such persecutors that they will even kill Christians because, as he says, "they have not known the Father ... or the Son."[9] One should notice in this connection that Aquinas does not here ascribe a lack of propositional knowledge about God

---

7   *Commentary on the Gospel of John*, Chapter 14, lecture 2, p. 57.

8   For a discussion of the connection between grace and an at least minimally moral condition, see my "The Non-Aristotelian Character of Aquinas's Ethics: Aquinas on the Passions," *Faith and Philosophy* 28.1 (2011), p. 29-43.

9   *Commentary on the Gospel of John*, Chapter 16, lecture 1, p. 132.

to these putative persecutors. What Aquinas says about them is that they lack personal knowledge of God: "they have not known *the Father*...."

On Aquinas's views of the New Testament's presentation of God, then, God's resemblance to Christ yields a certain kind of humanity about God, too. In seeing and knowing the incarnate Christ, who is fully human as well as divine, one sees and knows God the Father as well. Here, too, there is something that might be considered an anthropomorphism, in fact one that is given a metaphysically powerful presentation in the incarnation of Christ.

By contrast with these biblical representations of God, to many people the God of classical theism seems unresponsive, unengaged, and entirely inhuman. That is because, on classical theism as it is often interpreted, God is immutable, eternal, and simple, devoid of all potentiality, incapable of any passivity, and inaccessible to human knowledge. So described, the God of classical theism seems very different from the God of the Bible.

In various books and articles, I have argued for one or another claim that attempts to rebut this common attitude regarding the apparent inconsistency between the God of the Bible and the God of the philosophers. In this book, I try to lay out the case for the rejection of this inconsistency as fully as possible in order to show, with as much evidence and reason as can be mustered in one short book, that the God of classical theism is the engaged, personally present, responsive God of the Bible.

I will focus on just one proponent of classical theism, namely, Aquinas, because it is not possible to cover everything in this brief space and because Aquinas's work contains the representative classical theism that I know best. I will show that, for Aquinas, who is the most frequently invoked proponent of classical theism, an immutable, eternal, simple God is most certainly the God of the Bible, knowable, accessible, interactive with human beings, and responsive to them. For Aquinas, there is no inconsistency between the God of classical theism and the God of the Bible, not because the God of the Bible really is the frozen and remote deity some people take the God of classical theism to be, but because the God of classical theism really is the personal biblical God. As I will argue, the sense that the God of classical theism cannot be the God of the Bible is based on a mistaken understanding of the divine attributes at the heart of classical theism, at least in Aquinas's version of it.

The apparent inconsistency

Although the contemporary discussion of the apparent inconsistency between the God of the Bible and the God of classical theism has highlighted a variety of divine attributes standard in classical theism, I will focus here largely just on three: immutability, eternality, and simplicity, with its correlative notions that God lacks any potentiality or passivity and that God is incomprehensible to human beings.

(i) Immutability

The claim that God is immutable because God has no potentiality but is pure actuality has seemed to many philosophers and theologians to imply that God cannot be responsive to human beings, since nothing that a human person does or says could effect a change in such a God. An argument to this effect has been common with process philosophers. So, for instance, David Ray Griffin argues against the possibility that the God of classical theism could be responsive to human beings by highlighting what he sees as the implications of the claim that God is pure actuality and thus immutable. Griffin says, "*actus purus* is equatable with impassibility, for it implies that God does not have passive power, the power of being acted upon".[10]

As Griffin sees it, in order to be responsive, God would have to do something that he otherwise would not do, and he would have to do it because of something that a creature does. But if God is pure actuality, then it seems that God could not do anything because of what a creature does; responsiveness of this sort appears to require potentiality, which God lacks. That is, for God to be responsive to human beings, what God does would have to be a function

10 David Ray Griffin, *God, Power, and Evil: A Process Theodicy* (Philadelphia: Westminster Press, 1976), p.74; I am grateful to Theodore Vitali for this reference.

(at least in part) of what human beings do; but if God has no potentiality, then it seems that nothing about God could have its source in anything about human beings. The facts about God, one might say, are set, and nothing that human beings do can alter those facts.

Griffin is an opponent of classical theism, but even some of its proponents seem to share a view like Griffin's, except that, unlike Griffin, these proponents approve the conclusions they suppose that the doctrine of divine immutability leads to. The argument that no action of God's depends on anything done by human beings is maintained with vehemence by some defenders of classical theism, too.[11] So, for example, in discussing God's knowledge of human free choice, Reginald Garrigou-Lagrange says,

> God is either *determining* or *determined*, there is no other alternative... The knowledge of God is the CAUSE *of our free determinations,* or else it is CAUSED *by them... The knowledge of God either measures things or is measured by them.* Only anthropomorphism can admit the second term of the dilemma and therefore, from sheer necessity, we must keep to the first.[12]

The argument for this conclusion of Garrigou-Lagrange's is based on certain views of God's

11   I am grateful to Theodore Vitali for calling my attention to the need to address this argument explicitly.

12   Reginald Garrigou-Lagrange, *God, His Existence and Nature,* 5th ed., trans. Dom Bede Rose (St. Louis: Herder, 1955), p. 546-547.

immutability and consequent impassivity. So, for example, Garrigou-Lagrange says,

> one of the fundamental reasons... why every Thomist will always reject the Molinist theory [which is willing to accept "the second term of the dilemma" in the quotation above], is that this [Molinist] theory of necessity causes one to posit a *passivity in the pure Act.* If the divine causality is not *predetermining* with regard to our *choice...,* the divine knowledge is fatally *determined* by it. To wish to limit the universal causality and absolute independence of God, necessarily brings one to place a passivity in Him, a passivity in the *self-subsisting Being,* in the *self-subsisting Intellect.* If, in fact, the divine motion does not infallibly assure the execution of a divine intrinsically efficacious and predetermining decree, it follows, as Molina and his disciples maintain, that, *of two men equally tempted and EQUALLY HELPED by God,* it happens that one consents to co-operate with the grace and the other does not. And then the *difference,* which distinguishes the good from the bad consent and this man from that other, does not come from God, but *solely from man's free will....* It becomes consequently quite clear for one who speaks seriously and does not wish to trifle with words, that *the foreknowledge* is *passive* when one positively asserts that this *difference* does not at all come from God; just as I am a *passive* spectator *when I see* that this man, independently of me, is seated, whereas that other is standing... A new passivity has entered into the pure Act, who henceforth is no more like to God than is the false diamond like the true.... it is only *afterwards that God,* although He is Being itself,

Intelligence itself, Goodness itself, saw and willed it determinately. There is a twofold passivity in pure Act.[13]

Garrigou-Lagrange thus postulates a dilemma: for everything, either God determines it or he is determined by it, where determination for Garrigou-Lagrange is or is equivalent to causation, as the preceding texts make clear. And Garrigou-Lagrange argues for the first horn of the dilemma he constructs, namely, that God is always determining, on the grounds that the second horn of the dilemma, that sometimes God is responsive to what human beings choose to do, presupposes passivity, which cannot be in a God who is immutable and without potentiality. Garrigou-Lagrange goes so far as to apply this argument to God's knowledge. If God knows something because it exists or is the case, then there is passivity in "Intelligence itself," as Garrigou-Lagrange puts it. So, for Garrigou-Lagrange, even God's knowledge determines what God knows in virtue of the fact that it is the cause of everything that God knows.[14]

---

13   Garrigou-Lagrange 1955, p. 538-539.

14   This conclusion obviously cannot stand if the object of God's knowledge is anything about God's existence or nature. So, for example, God's knowledge of his existence manifestly cannot be the cause of God's existence. But even when it comes to God's knowledge of creatures, the conclusion is not only false but taken to be false by Garrigou-Lagrange's chief source for classical theism, Aquinas. So, for example, if a person's morally wrong actions occur in virtue of the causal efficacy of God's knowledge, then God who causes them in virtue of

By the same token, on Garrigou-Lagrange's view, if God

knowing them is also responsible for them. On Garrigou-Lagrange's interpretation, then, it is God who would be the ultimate cause, and so the ultimate agent, of morally wrong human actions, just in virtue of knowing them. Apart from the obvious religious difficulties of this conclusion, it has the additional unhappy result that it makes Aquinas blatantly contradict himself, since Aquinas also maintains that God is not the cause of human evil. (See, for example, *Quaestiones Disputatae de Veritate* (QDV) 2.15; also, ST I-II q.79 a.1.) (For references and further discussion of these points, see my and Norman Kretzmann's "Eternity and God's Knowledge: A Reply to Shanley", *American Catholic Philosophical Quarterly* 72 [1998], p. 439-445.) In addition, for Aquinas God's knowledge of future contingents is crucially tied to God's eternality. It is clear from many passages in Aquinas's work that Aquinas supposes God knows future contingents in virtue of their being present to him in his eternity. But, on Garrigou-Lagrange's view of God's knowledge, God knows a state of affairs just because he causes it to be. God's knowledge of future contingents, then, should be explainable for Aquinas just as God's knowledge of anything else is: as a function of the causal efficacy of the divine cognition. In fact, there should be no special problem about God's knowledge of future contingents. Consequently, the doctrine of divine eternity would be irrelevant to an explanation of God's knowledge of future contingents. There is not only no need for the doctrine of eternity in explanations of God's knowledge of future contingents on Garrigou-Lagrange's interpretation, there is not even a role for it. But, in fact, Aquinas clearly thinks that God's knowledge of future contingents needs to be explained in some special way, in terms of divine eternality.

wills something because of something creatures do, there is yet another sort of passivity in God, namely, in God's will. Consequently, for Garrigou-Lagrange, God's will is a cause of everything in creation, but it does not depend on anything in creation.

Therefore, Garrigou-Lagrange supposes, God cannot do anything in response to what creatures do. Presumably, God can do something because of something else that God himself does; that is, God can will that there is an answer to Jonah's prayer because God wills that Jonah prays for rescue from drowning. But, on Garrigou-Lagrange's position, God cannot will Jonah's rescue because of Jonah's prayer; and he cannot know Jonah's prayer because Jonah makes it. If he did, God would know and will what he does because of something that a creature does. In that case, according to Garrigou-Lagrange, God would be determined, instead of determining, and there would be passivity in God, as there cannot be on the view that God is immutable and lacks all potentiality.

So for detractors of classical theism and also some adherents of it, it seems that an immutable God could not answer prayer, as Jonah's God does, because what an immutable God knows or wills cannot be dependent on what a human being does; and so, it seems, God's decisions cannot be altered by human prayer or be in any other way responsive to

---

For a view of God's knowledge very different from that of Garrigou-Lagrange, see Stump 2003, Chapter 5.

it. A fortiori, since an immutable God cannot change his mind or retract a previously made decision, it seems that an immutable God could not first decide to destroy a city and then decide not to do so because of the actions of the people in that city.

It seems, then, that the doctrine of immutability implies that the God of classical theism cannot be the God of the Bible.

(ii) Eternity

Eternity implies immutability. On the doctrine of eternity, God is outside time; but change requires succession, which is characteristic of time, and so nothing that is outside time can change. Consequently, many of the problems highlighted above in connection with an immutable God apply also to an eternal God. In addition, however, the claim that God is eternal has seemed to some contemporary philosophers and theologians to raise special problems of its own because it seems to imply that God cannot engage in second-personal interaction with human beings, as, for example, conversation requires. On this view, nothing that is outside of time could engage interactively with a person inside time.

So, for example, William Hasker has argued that an eternal God could not be directly aware of temporal facts or personally engaged with temporal creatures.[15] In particular, God could not be with

---

15   "One can be immediately aware only of what is *present* for one to be aware of; what else, after all, can 'immediate'

human beings directly and immediately, in the way God seems to be with Jonah. An eternal God could observe human beings and see them as present to him, but an eternal God could not be with them in anything analogous to face-to-face connection. In effect, Hasker supposes that to be directly aware of temporal beings and so directly engaged with them requires being temporal oneself. And so Hasker concludes that classical theism requires the rejection of the God of the Bible, who is personally present to his people.

Hasker's objection to the doctrine of divine eternity is the mirror image of one raised by Delmas Lewis.[16] Lewis argues that if temporal beings are really present to an eternal being, they must be present in that being's mode of existence; that is, they must themselves be eternal. Otherwise, Lewis thinks, they will be only epistemically and not also metaphysically present to an eternal God. But since what is temporal cannot also be eternal, then, according to Lew-

---

mean? If God is timeless, he can be immediately aware of (supposedly) temporal facts only if these facts *really are* timeless after all. If, on the other hand, the world really is temporal, only a temporal God can be immediately aware of it—and then only of its *present*, not of its past or future" (William Hasker, *God, Time, and Knowledge* [Ithaca and London: Cornell University Press, 1989], p. 169). For a different understanding of 'immediate' with regard to awareness and presence, see Stump 2010, Chapter 4.

16   "Eternity, Time and Tenselessness," *Faith and Philosophy* 5 (1988), p. 72-86.

is, the doctrine of God's eternity has the unwelcome consequence that temporal beings are only epistemically and not really, metaphysically, present to God.

In the view of such philosophers, then, an eternal God could produce timeless decrees, but such a God could not answer Jonah after Jonah has prayed to God; and, in general, such a God could not be personally engaged in conversation with a human person, as God is with Jonah in the story.

And so, in virtue of implying metaphysical distance between God and creatures, the doctrine of divine eternity apparently also implies that the God of classical theism cannot be the God of the Bible.

(iii) Simplicity

Finally, the claim that God is simple has seemed to some contemporary philosophers and theologians to imply that, at best, human beings can have no positive knowledge of God and that, at worst, God is entirely unknowable by human beings.

So, for example, in presenting Aquinas's position on human knowledge of God, David Burrell says, "That God's nature, otherwise utterly unknown, must be affirmed simply to be, gives a warrant of sorts for taking to-be as an act."[17]

Elsewhere he says,

---

17   David Burrell, *Aquinas: God and Action* (Notre Dame: University of Notre Dame Press, 1979), p. 139.

> We cannot speak of God at all… [on Aquinas's theory
> of divine simplicity] unless it be under the rubric of
> 'the first cause of all.' Yet such a cause leaves no proper
> traces since its *modus operandi* cannot conform to the
> ordinary patterns whereby effect resembles cause…
> In the measure, then, that our language embodies a
> subject/predicate, genus/species grammar…, no de-
> scription can succeed in identifying a trace of divinity.[18]

And he sums up his position by saying, "properly
speaking, nothing can be said of God."[19]

Leo Elders puts the point even more explicitly:

> The comprehension of God's essence is altogether
> excluded. This conclusion is presupposed in the
> Prologue to the Third Question [of Aquinas's *Summa
> theologiae*]…. Even if we say that God is perfect, good
> or eternal, we must realize that we do not know what
> these terms mean when predicated of God."[20]

Claims such as these can give the impression that,
for classical theism, because of God's simplicity, it is
not possible for human beings to have any positive
knowledge of God. On this interpretation of divine
simplicity, Aquinas apparently maintains that because
God is simple, human beings can know what God is
not, but they cannot know anything positive regarding

---

18   Burrell 1979, p. 60-61.

19   Burrell 1979, p. 25.

20   Leo Elders, *The Philosophical Theology of St. Thomas
      Aquinas* (Leiden: E.J. Brill, 1990), p. 143.

any attribute of God's.[21] Unlike Jonah in the story, no human being (at least in this life) could know a simple God or be engaged in inter-personal conversation with God. The anthropomorphism of the God who talks to Jonah looks antithetical to the incomprehensibility of a simple God.

Even worse, the view of divine simplicity held by many of its adherents (and many of its detractors too) seems to imply that God is only *being* itself, *esse* alone, and not an entity or a being (an *id quod est*) at all. So, for example, explicating a position he thinks is at least continuous with that of Aquinas, Lorenz Puntel describes the God of Aquinas as "Being, not *a being*, because its status is absolutely unique. It is not an additional being, not even a (or the) first or highest being."[22] Elders says, "For St. Thomas God is never 'an object', for God is far above our understanding."[23] Similarly, Burrell says, "God is not an object.... Ordinary objective discourse...betrays rather than displays God's way of being."[24] And Brian Davies says, "[God] is not like anything we know.

---

21   For discussion of this position in the secondary literature, see Stump 2003, Chapter 3.

22   Lorenz Puntel, *Being and God. A Systematic Approach in Confrontation with Martin Heidegger, Emmanuel Levinas, and Jean-Luc Marion*, trans. Alan White (Evanston, Illinois: Northwestern University Press, 2011), p. 236.

23   Leo Elders, *The Philosophical Theology of St. Thomas Aquinas* (Leiden: E.J. Brill, 1990), p. 22.

24   Burrell 1979, p. 25.

...God is... not an individual.... For this reason it surely makes sense to call him incomprehensible."[25] But if God is not a being at all, not any kind of concrete particular, it is hard to see how a human person could have a personal relationship to God and engage in conversation with him, as Jonah does in the story.

So understood, then, the God of classical theism has seemed to many opponents of classical theism to be not only unbiblical but even religiously pernicious. In his own Aquinas lecture, Alvin Plantinga puts this conclusion in terms of God's being a property, but his objections remain the same if we transpose 'property' into 'esse'. Plantinga says, "This view [that God is identical to a property alone] is subject to a difficulty both obvious and overwhelming. No property could have created the world; no property could be omniscient, or, indeed, know anything at all."[26]

And Plantinga summarizes the problem in a way that is apt for my purposes here. He says, "If God is a property, then he isn't a person..."[27]

We do not need to worry whether a triune God can be thought of as *a person* in order to see the power of Plantinga's complaint. Even on the doctrine of the

---

25   Brian Davies, *The Reality of God and the Problem of Evil* (London: Continuum, 2006), p. 78-79.

26   Alvin Plantinga, *Does God Have a Nature?* (Milwaukee: Marquette University Press, 1980), p. 47.

27   Plantinga 1980, p. 47.

Trinity, which takes God to consist in three persons (where 'person' has a technical, theological sense), God is characterized by one mind and one will. Anything with a mind and a will, however, is an entity, an *id quod est*. For this reason, Plantinga is right to say that if God is only a property—or only *esse*—then God is not a person, in our sense of the word 'person' as something with both mind and will. Nothing that is not an entity at all could have a mind and a will (or be a something characterizable by mind and will). Nothing that is not even an entity could enter into any kind of personal relationship with human persons. In fact, it seems that *no* standard divine attributes such as *being omniscient* or *being possessed of free will*, for example, could apply to something that is not a being. Or, to put the same point another way, it is very hard to see how something which is not a being but which is characterized only as *being* itself could be capable of knowing or loving anything.

As far as that goes, nothing that is not a being could act at all. As Aquinas himself is at pains to show in his commentary on Boethius's *De hebdomadibus*, only an entity, an *id quod est*, can engage in action.[28] Expressing a similar thought, Davies says,

> The thought of God intervening in the created order (or intruding into it) is an exceedingly odd one. It would not be so if we took God to be an agent akin to a

28   See my "God's Simplicity," in *The Oxford Handbook of Aquinas*, ed. Brian Davies and Eleonore Stump (Oxford: Oxford University Press, 2012), p. 135-146.

human being... Such an agent might well be thought of as able to intervene... Yet God... is not such an agent. I take God to be the cause of the existence of everything other than himself, and it seems hard to see how God, so understood, can be thought of as literally able to intervene or to interfere with what he brings about.[29]

Furthermore, if God is only *being* and not a being, then God has no accidents and no essential properties either. He is only *esse*, and nothing else. Consequently, if we ascribe to God attributes such as free choice that are required for personal interaction, the result is incoherence. Even if we bracket the problem stemming from the claim that God has no accidents, on the interpretation of God as only *esse*, ascribing to God free choice yields a deep and irreducible difference among God's characteristics, contrary to the doctrine of simplicity, which maintains that God's nature is indivisibly one. If God has free choice, then some of the things characterizing God are things God chooses to be characterized by—such as his being a God who creates. But it makes no sense to suppose that God freely chooses all the things that characterize him, so that it is up to him, for example, whether or not he is immutable, eternal, and simple. So on interpretations of simplicity that take God to be *esse* alone, there will be a distinction between two groups of things characterizing God: those that are freely chosen by God and those regarding which God has no choice. And this apparently real distinction among things

---

29   Davies 2006, p. 75.

characterizing God cannot be explained as only a reflection of diversity in the temporal effects brought about by the single eternal activity which is God, or as no more than different manifestations of a single action. Instead, this distinction appears to express a radical diversity within the divine nature itself, in that some characteristics of God—such as his existing—are not subject to his control, while others—presumably such as his creating the world—are consequences of his free choice.[30]

---

30   This apparent diversity is clearly expressed by Aquinas in such passages as these:

> God necessarily wills his own being and his own goodness, and he *cannot* [my emphasis] will the contrary (*SCG* I.80);

> in respect of himself God has only volition, but in respect of other things he has selection (*electio*). Selection, however, is always accomplished by means of free choice. Therefore, free choice is suited to God (*SCG* I.88);

> free choice is spoken of in respect of things one wills *not* [my emphasis] necessarily but of one's own accord (*SCG* I.88).

(For SCG, I like and therefore have used the translation of Anton Pegis, but I have modified it in those few cases where I thought I could do better. The page references given below to SCG are to the Pegis translation: Aquinas, *Summa contra Gentiles*, trans. Anton Charles Pegis [Notre Dame: Notre Dame University Press, 1975].) Notice that

And so it seems as if divine simplicity rules out even free choice in God. A simple God apparently could not choose to interact with Jonah or choose to respond to his prayer, as the God of the story of Jonah does.

The doctrine of simplicity, then, seems to imply that the God of classical theism cannot be the God of the Bible.

(iv) The problem summarized

Although, for brevity's sake, I have framed the statement of the problem in the preceding sections in terms of the story of Jonah, the same points apply, mutatis mutandis, with regard to the God of the New Testament, too, on the kind of view of Christ Aquinas and many contemporary interpreters adopt. And so, to some contemporary philosophers and theologians, the God of the Bible looks nothing like the God of classical theism. How could the God who was so present and responsive to Jonah be the immutable, eternal, simple God of classical theism? How could such a God be seen and known in the human Christ?

Think of the problem this way. The biblical God is able and willing to enter into second-personal relationships. In the biblical stories, human beings can say 'you' to God; and the biblical God is able to say 'you' in return, not only to human beings but also

---

even though God's existence and attributes are conceived of here as being *willed* by God, they are expressly excluded from among the objects of God's free choice.

to the sea beasts (as in Jonah) and to trees (Mark 11:14) and even to the sea (Job 38:11).

When in the book of Job God is determining the extent of the sea, it is notable that he does so by *talking* to it. God does not just wield his great power to decree what the nature and attributes of a sea must be. Presumably, God could do so with an act of will alone, without making any utterances. Or, if he wanted to determine what the sea did by means of an utterance, God could make an impersonal statement, addressed to no one in particular, of this sort: 'I decree that the sea will extend from here to there, but it will not extend any further.' Instead, what we get in the description of God's determination of the extent of the sea is an account of a second-personal interaction between God and the sea. God addresses the sea directly, in second-person forms of speech. In fact, God talks to the sea as if the sea were a rambunctious and exuberant child of his, but nonetheless a child who can hear him, understand him, and respond to him.

Analogously, in the New Testament, when Christ goes to a fig tree hungry and finds no figs on it, he intends that the non-productive fig tree wither. Christ could produce this withering by a simple internal and tacit act of will, as in another story he turns water into wine. But instead Christ effects the end he intends by speaking directly to the tree in second-personal terms of address. Jesus produces the withering of the tree by saying to the tree, "Let no one eat fruit of *you* (emphasis added) after this forever!" (Mark 11:14).

And now the problem is evident. How could *being* say 'you' to anything? And who could use second-personal address in any locution towards God if God is *being* alone? And, in general, in the biblical stories, there is a readily discernible image of God in human beings, and conversely a readily discernible divine original in God for the image of God in human beings. By contrast, there seems to be so little in common between God and human beings on the characterization of the God of classical theism as I have described it here that it is hard to imagine why anyone would suppose that human beings are made in the image of such a God.

In the Christian world, classical theism held sway for well over a millennium, in a tradition that ranges from the thought of Augustine (and earlier) to that of Aquinas (and later). Augustine and Aquinas both certainly accept the divine attributes central to the characterization of God in classical theism as I sketched it above: immutability, eternity, and simplicity. And yet it is noteworthy that each of these great thinkers also wrote biblical commentaries without giving any indication of unease at the combination of biblical stories and classical theism. What is even more noteworthy is that each of them supposes that the engaged, knowable, personally present, responsive God of the biblical stories is available to him personally. In his *Confessions*, for example, Augustine addresses God directly, in second-personal terms, and he clearly assumes that God is available and responsive to him. A similar point can be made about Aquinas. In all his works, but especially in his biblical commentaries, he shows that he expects God to be engaged with all human beings, himself included, in such a way that God is known by human beings and is personally present and responsive to them.

How is it possible that these and other philosophers and theologians in the tradition of classical theism could also have accepted the picture of God in the biblical stories? Is it so much as metaphysically possible for the God of classical theism to be the God of the biblical stories?

I want to approach these questions by what may seem a circuitous route. I will begin by sketching Aquinas's views of the Holy Spirit and his account of the gifts and fruits of the Holy Spirit when it indwells in a person of faith. On Christian doctrine, which Aquinas certainly accepts, the Holy Spirit is God; all the characteristics of God are also the characteristics of the Holy Spirit. That is, if God is immutable, so is the Holy Spirit; and the same point applies to the other attributes characterizing the God of classical theism, including eternity and simplicity. If God is eternal or simple, then so is the Holy Spirit; on the doctrine of the Trinity, it could not be that the Holy Spirit is temporal or composite while God is eternal and simple.[31] And so whatever Aquinas accepts as true of the Holy Spirit is also true of God. I will argue that, on Aquinas's views of the Holy Spirit, God is as intimately and responsively engaged with human beings, as knowable and personally present to human beings, as any proponent of the characterization of the biblical God could want. There is no difficulty in seeing that the God of the biblical story of Jonah could be the God Aquinas describes in his account of the Holy Spirit's interactions with human beings.

On the other hand, of course, in the history of Christian thought, Aquinas is one of the most influential proponents of classical theism. So in the next sections of this book, I will show why Aquinas's account of the Holy Spirit is compatible with his view of God as immutable, eternal, and simple. Contrary to some contemporary interpretations of classical theism, nothing about these divine attributes as Aquinas understands them rules out the characteristics and relations Aquinas attributes to the Holy Spirit. Consequently, both the questions

---

31 Some contemporary scholars suppose that the doctrine of the Trinity is incompatible with the doctrine of divine simplicity. For an argument that the doctrine of the Trinity *requires* the doctrine of divine simplicity, see Thomas Joseph White, "Divine Simplicity and the Holy Trinity," *International Journal of Systematic Theology* (forthcoming), and "Nicene Orthodoxy and Trinitarian Simplicity," *American Catholic Philosophical Quarterly* (forthcoming).

above have an answer. Aquinas accepted the picture of God given in the biblical stories because it did not contradict his own classical theist view of God. And he was right in this assessment. As I will try to show, nothing about God's immutability, eternality, or simplicity, as Aquinas interprets these divine attributes, precludes any of the characteristics of the biblical God.

Aquinas on the Holy Spirit

To show the way in which Aquinas thinks of the relations between God and human beings that are mediated by the Holy Spirit, it is helpful to begin with Aquinas's exposition of the characteristics of the Holy Spirit.

The very name of the Holy Spirit, as Aquinas explains it, is indicative of Aquinas's views. When Aquinas describes the Holy Spirit in the *Summa theologiae* (ST), he says that the name of the person of the Holy Spirit is 'Gift'. In saying this, he is validating a claim of Augustine's: "the gift of the Holy Spirit is nothing but the Holy Spirit".[32] To explain this claim, Aquinas says,

---

32 ST I q.38 a.1 s.c. I like and therefore have used the translations from *Summa Theologica*, trans. by the Fathers of the English Dominican Province (reprinted by Christian Classics, 1981), but I have felt free to modify those translations in the few places where I felt I could do better.

We are said to possess what we can freely use or enjoy as we please.... A rational creature does sometimes attain to this, ... so as freely to know God truly and to love God rightly. Hence, rational creatures alone can possess the divine person.. [But] this must be given to a rational creature from God, for that is said to be given to us which we have from another source. And so a divine person can be given and can be a gift.[33]

Aquinas goes on to say, "the divine person is called 'Gift' from eternity, but he is given in time."[34] Elsewhere he approves Augustine's line, "the Holy Spirit proceeds temporally for the creature's sanctification." And he adds, "So the sending of the Holy Spirit is a temporal procession. The Holy Spirit is sent in the sense that he exists newly in any one, and he is given when he is possessed by anyone."[35]

Aquinas expands on these views this way:

God is in all things by his essence, power, and presence, according to his one common mode, as the cause existing in the effects which participate in his goodness. In addition to this common mode, however, there is one special mode belonging to the rational nature in whom God is said to be present as the object known is in the knower and the beloved in the lover. Since by its operation of knowledge and love a rational creature attains to God himself, then according to this special mode God is said not only to exist in a rational

---

33   ST I q.38 a.1 corpus.

34   ST I q.38 a.1 ad 4.

35   ST I q.43 a.3 s.c. and corpus.

creature but also to dwell in that rational creature as in his own temple.[36]

In many other places, Aquinas expresses similar views. So, for example, he says,

> We are said to possess only what we can freely use or enjoy; and to have the power of enjoying the divine person can only be according to sanctifying grace. And yet the Holy Spirit is possessed by human beings and dwells within them, in the very gift of sanctifying grace. For this reason, the Holy Spirit himself is given.[37]

And in a reply to an objection in this same question, he adds, "By the gift of sanctifying grace, a rational creature is perfected so that it can not only freely use the created gift [of grace] but also enjoy the divine person himself…. And so the divine person himself is given."[38]

In *Summa contra Gentiles* (SCG), Aquinas makes clear that, in his view, God himself, the whole Trinity, indwells a person of faith when that person has the indwelling Holy Spirit:

> Since the love by which we love God is in us by the Holy Spirit, the Holy Spirit himself must also be in us… Therefore, since we are made lovers of God by the Holy Spirit, and every beloved is in the lover…by

---

36   ST I q.43 a.3 corpus.

37   ST I q.43 a.3 corpus.

38   ST I q.43 a.3 ad 1.

the Holy Spirit necessarily the Father and the Son dwell in us also.[39]

In addition, for Aquinas, a person is justified by faith when she ceases resisting God, and God in consequence gives her the grace that produces faith in her.[40] According to Aquinas, this transition is

---

39   SCG IV c.21, p.122.

40   As Aquinas sees it, a fully functional adult human being in a post-Fall condition who is not converted or in the process of being converted refuses grace continually, even if she is not aware of doing so. Before she is justified, she has a resistance or disinclination towards the second-order volition in which sinners detest their sin and long for God's goodness, the act of will towards which the providence of God urges her. At some point, however, her refusal of grace may be quelled. But the quelling of refusal is not equivalent to assent. A person can cease to refuse grace without assenting to it, on Aquinas's views. Instead, she can just be quiescent in will. If she is, then God, who offers grace to every human being, immediately infuses in her the previously refused grace; God avails himself of the absence of refusal on her part to produce in her the good will of justifying faith. Consequently, it is possible to hold consistently both that the will of faith, like any good will whatsoever in a human being, is brought about only by God's grace, but that a human being is still ultimately in control of the state of her will, insofar as it is up to her either to refuse grace or to fail to refuse grace, and God's giving of grace depends on the state of her will. Nonetheless, all forms of Pelagianism are avoided since nothing in these claims requires Aquinas to give up the view that there

instantaneous; that is, a person comes to this faith in an instant, a datable, discernible instant. So, for example, Aquinas says,

> when some mean must be recognized between the endpoints of a change, the transition from one endpoint to another must be successive, because that which is moved continuously must first be changed to the mean before it is changed to the final endpoint....But when there cannot be a mean between the two endpoints of a change or motion... , then the transition from one endpoint to the other does not occur in [a period of] time but rather in an instant. And this happens when the two endpoints of a motion or change are ... privation and form. ... And so I say that the endpoints of justification are grace and the privation of grace. Between these there is no mean... and therefore the

is nothing good in a human person's will which is not produced in it by God's grace. Because ultimate control over the state of her will is vested in the person being justified, Aquinas's account (on this interpretation of it) can give an answer to the question Augustine wrestled with, namely, why God does not cause the justifying act of will in everyone. Whether or not God causes that act of will in a person is dependent on whether or not that person's will has ceased to reject grace, and that is something for which she herself is ultimately responsible. Furthermore, since a human being not only is ultimately responsible for her state of will but also has alternative possibilities with regard to willing, it does seem right to hold, as (on this interpretation) Aquinas does, that the justifying act of will is a free act, and even free in a libertarian sense. For detailed discussion of these issues, see Stump 2003, Chapters 12 and 13.

transition from one to the other is in an instant ...
And so the whole justification of an impious person
occurs in an instant....[41]

The reasons behind this theological position are
metaphysical and complex and need not concern us
now.[42] For my purposes here, what is important is only
that Aquinas takes justifying faith to be faith informed
by love or *caritas*; and he supposes that both faith and
love are infused by God in the instant in which a person
comes to faith. In fact, Aquinas holds a unity of the
virtues thesis, and so he maintains that in the instant
at which a person comes to faith, "all the moral virtues
are infused simultaneously together with love."[43]

In that same instant, on Aquinas's views, the Holy
Spirit itself comes to dwell in the person who receives grace and faith. Not only does she receive in
that instant all the virtues (in some nascent degree)
but she also receives God himself in the person of
the Holy Spirit. And when the Holy Spirit comes to
indwell in her, it also confers on her at the same time
all the gifts and fruits of the Holy Spirit.

41　QDV 28.9 reply. Translations from QDV are my own,
although I consulted the helpful translation by Robert
Schmidt (*Truth. St. Thomas Aquinas,* [Indianapolis, IN:
Hackett Publishing Co., reprinted 1994).

42　For some explanation of the metaphysics, see the
discussion of the difference between efficient causation
and formal causation with regard to God's giving of grace
to the will in Stump 2003, Chapter 13.

43　ST I-II q.65 a.3.

For Aquinas, the infused virtues are the only real virtues,[44] and they are necessary for the moral life. Nonetheless, the real heart of the moral life lies in the gifts and fruits of the Holy Spirit. It is not possible, on Aquinas's view, to have one's rational faculties of intellect and will be in a morally good state without the indwelling Holy Spirit and the gifts and fruits that the Holy Spirit brings with it.[45] On the contrary, salvation requires all the gifts of the Holy Spirit. So, for example, commenting on texts which imply that two of the gifts, wisdom and fear of the Lord, are required for salvation, Aquinas says, "Of all the gifts, wisdom seems to be the highest, and fear the lowest. Now each of these is necessary for salvation…. Therefore the other gifts that are placed between these are also necessary for salvation."[46]

Therefore, in the first instant of faith, every person of faith comes to have the infused virtues, the gifts and fruits of the Holy Spirit, and the Holy Spirit itself indwelling in her.[47] And, in this instant, the divine indwelling unites that human person with God to some (no doubt limited) degree. In so doing, it

---

44   In this connection, the infused virtues are distinguished from the acquired or Aristotelian virtues, which have some of the character of virtue but do not fit the complete definition of virtue.

45   See, for example, ST I-II q. 68 a.2.

46   ST I-II q.68 a.2 s.c.

47   For a detailed defense of these claims, see Stump 2011.

makes God available to her to know, to love, and to enjoy.

This is a position Aquinas maintains and develops in many places. So, for example, in commenting on Paul's wish for the Ephesians, "that you may able to comprehend, with all the saints, what is the breadth and length and height and depth [of the love of God]," Aquinas says,

> It is evident from John 14:21 that God reveals himself to one who loves.. and that he shows himself to one who believes.... Now it should be noted that sometimes to comprehend means 'to enclose', and then it is necessary that the one comprehending totally contains within himself what is comprehended. But sometimes it means 'to apprehend', and then it affirms a remoteness or a distance and yet implies proximity. No created intellect can comprehend God in the first manner...But the second kind [of comprehension] is one of the gifts [of the Holy Spirit], and this is what the Apostle means when he says [to the Ephesians] 'that you may comprehend'—namely, that you may enjoy the presence of God and know him intimately.[48]

In Romans 5:5, Paul says "the love of God is poured forth in our hearts by the Holy Spirit who is given

---

48   *Commentary on Ephesians*, Chapter 3, lecture 5. I like and therefore have used the translations from *Commentary on Saint Paul's Epistle to the Ephesians* by St. Thomas Aquinas, trans. Matthew L. Lamb (Albany: Magi Books, 1966), but I have felt free to modify those translations in the few places where I felt I could do better. Page references below are to their translation.

to us". In one of the many places in which Aquinas comments on this line, he says,

> The love of God can be taken in two ways. In one way, for the love by which God loves us…; in another way for the love by which we love God…. Both these loves of God are poured into our hearts by the Holy Spirit who has been given to us. For the Holy Spirit… to be given to us is our being brought to participate in the love who is the Holy Spirit. [49]

In his commentary on the Gospel of John, Aquinas characterizes the relation of the Holy Spirit to the person in whom the Spirit dwells in this way: "The Father … will give the Holy Spirit, who is the Consoler, since he is the Spirit of love. It is love that causes spiritual consolation and joy…."[50]

In commenting on a line in Ephesians, where Paul says that the Ephesians have the promise of the Holy Spirit (Ephesians 1:13), Aquinas says, "The Holy Spirit is given with a certain promise, since by the very fact that he is given to us we become the

---

49   *Commentary on Romans*, Chapter 5, lecture 1. I like and therefore have used the translation in *St. Thomas Aquinas. Commentary on the Letter of St. Paul to the Romans*, trans. F. R. Larcher, ed. J. Mortensen and F. Alarcon (Lander, Wyoming: The Aquinas Institute for the Study of Sacred Doctrine, 2012); this quotation is found on p. 132.

50   *Commentary on the Gospel of John*, Chapter 14, lecture 4, p. 70.

children of God. For through the Holy Spirit we are made one with Christ".[51]

For Aquinas, then, the relationship between God and a human person of faith which is brought about through the indwelling of the Holy Spirit is one that is close enough and intimate enough to be thought of as a uniting in love.

The gifts and fruits of the Holy Spirit are an important part of this relationship. To see something of the nature of the gifts, take, for example, courage. On Aquinas's account, courage can be considered as an infused virtue or as a gift of the Holy Spirit. Courage considered as an infused virtue is a disposition which is infused into a person by God and which makes that person suitable for the community of heaven.[52] Considered in this way, courage is a real virtue, but it is not courage in its full form. For courage in its full form, one needs courage as a gift of the Holy Spirit. Considered as a gift, however, courage is very different from courage as an infused virtue. Taken as a gift, courage is a disposition to act on the settled conviction that one is united to God now and will be united to God in heaven when one dies.[53]

---

51   *Commentary on Ephesians*, Chapter 1, lecture 5, p. 66.

52   For the general discussion, see *Quaestiones disputatae de virtutibus in communi* q. un. a.9 and *Quaestiones disputatae de virtutibus cardinalibus*, q. un. a.2. Cf. also ST II-II q. 124 a.2 ad 1, and q.123 a.5, 6, and 7 and q.140 a.1.

53   See, for example, ST II-II q. 139 a.1.

Considered as a gift, courage, like the rest of the gifts, has its source in relationship with God, whose indwelling Holy Spirit unites a human person to God in love. By filling a person with joy in love with God, Aquinas says, the Holy Spirit protects people against two kinds of evils, which might otherwise make them give way to fear:

> [it protects them] first against the evil which disturbs peace, since peace is disturbed by adversities. But with regard to adversities the Holy Spirit perfects [people] through patience, which enables [them] to bear adversities patiently. . . . Second, [it protects them] against the evil which arrests joy, namely, the wait for what is loved. To this evil, the Spirit opposes long-suffering, which is not broken by the waiting.[54]

The gift of courage in the face of adversity is thus one result stemming from the indwelling Holy Spirit and the union in love that the indwelling Holy Spirit brings with it.

There are seven gifts which the indwelling Holy Spirit brings to a person of faith; these are *pietas,*

---

54   Aquinas, *Commentary on Galatians,* Chapter 5, lecture 6. There is an English translation of this work: *Commentary on Saint Paul's Epistle to the Galatians by St. Thomas Aquinas,* trans. F. R. Larcher and Richard Murphy (Albany: Magi Books, 1966). Although I have preferred to use my own translations, I found the Larcher and Murphy translation helpful. For this passage, see Larcher and Murphy, p. 180. Cf. also, *Commentary on Hebrews,* Chapter 12, lecture 2.

courage, fear of the Lord, wisdom, understanding, counsel, and knowledge. Each of the seven gifts has an analogue among the infused virtues, from which the gifts are to be distinguished. In explaining why the gifts of the Holy Spirit are greater than their analogues among the infused virtues, Aquinas says,

> These perfections are called 'gifts', not only because they are infused by God, but also because by them a human being is disposed to become amenable to the divine inspiration... for those who are moved by divine inspiration, there is no need to take counsel according to human reason, but only to follow their inner promptings, since they are moved by a principle higher than human reason.[55]

And elsewhere Aquinas says about the gifts that "[they] are habits perfecting a human being so that he is ready to follow the promptings of the Holy Spirit..."[56]

The idea that the Holy Spirit who is within a person of faith speaks to that person interiorly or is otherwise in communication within that person is one that Aquinas puts forward in many places. So, for example, Aquinas says, "the gifts, as distinct from the infused virtues, may be defined as something given by God in relation to his motion, that is, as something that makes a human being follow well the promptings of God."[57]

---

55   ST I-II q.68 a.1 corpus.

56   ST I-II q.68 a. 4 corpus.

57   ST I-II q.68 a.1 ad 3.

It is worth noting in this connection that four of the gifts of the Holy Spirit are gifts for the intellect. In his commentary on the Gospel of John, Aquinas describes the sending of the Holy Spirit to a person of faith this way: "the effect of this kind of sending is to make us sharers in the divine wisdom and know-ers of the truth.... The Spirit makes us know all things by inspiring us from within, by directing us and lifting us up to spiritual things."[58]

And in SCG IV c.22, Aquinas gives this claim a powerful extension: "Since by the Holy Spirit we are established as friends of God, fittingly enough it is by the Holy Spirit that human beings are said to re-ceive the revelation of the divine mysteries."[59]

Expanding on the idea that a person of faith is friends with God, Aquinas says:

> In the first place, it is proper to friendship to converse with one's friend.... It is also a property of friendship that one take delight in a friend's presence, that one rejoice in his words and deeds... and it is especially in our sorrows that we hasten to our friends for consolation. Since then the Holy Spirit constitutes us God's friends and makes God dwell in us and us dwell in God, it follows that through the Holy Spirit we have joy in God.[60]

---

58   *Commentary on the Gospel of John*, Chapter 14, lecture 6, p. 87.

59   SCG IV c.22, p.123.

60   SCG IV c.23, p.125-126.

Finally, the fruits of the Holy Spirit are love, joy, peace, patience, long-suffering, goodness, benevolence, mildness, fidelity, modesty, continence, and chastity. About these, Aquinas says,

> Among the fruits of the Holy Spirit, we count love, since the Holy Spirit himself is love. And that is why it is written (Rom.5:5): 'The love of God is poured forth in our hearts by the Holy Spirit who is given to us.' The necessary result of [this] love ... is joy, because every lover rejoices at being united to the beloved. Now love has always the actual presence of God whom it loves... and that is why the consequence of love is joy. And the perfection of joy is peace... [61]

In fact, for Aquinas, the Holy Spirit so fills a person with a sense of the love of God and God's presence to him that joy is one of the principal effects of the Holy Spirit.[62] Aquinas says, "When [Paul] says 'the Lord is near,' he points out the cause of joy, because a person rejoices at the nearness of his friend."[63]

So, on Aquinas's views, a person of faith will have as present as possible, not only with himself but even within himself, the God who is his beloved. That is

---

61   ST I-II q.70 a.3 corpus.

62   See, for example, *Commentary on Romans,* Chapter 5, lecture 1.

63   *Commentary on Philippians,* Chapter 4, lecture 1. For the English translation, see *Commentary on Saint Paul's First Letter to the Thessalonians and the Letter to the Philippians by St. Thomas Aquinas,* trans. F. R. Larcher and Michael Duffy (Albany: Magi Books, 1969), p. 113.

why the list of the fruits of this union begins with love, joy, and peace --- love, because his beloved, who loves him, is present to him; joy, because of the dynamic interaction with his beloved, who is present to him in second-personal ways; and peace, because his heart already has what it most desires, his beloved, present to him.[64] As Aquinas explains it, there is no faith, no life of grace, without the indwelling Holy Spirit, with its concomitant love, joy, peace, and the other fruits of this union. The indwelling of the Holy Spirit is not reserved for the spiritually advanced, the saints and mystics; it is found in all people of faith.

Consequently, according to Aquinas's account of the indwelling Holy Spirit, for every person of faith, the immutable, eternal, simple Holy Spirit, who is God, is present, with mutual knowledge, mutual speech, and mutual love. It is evident, then, that the God described in Aquinas's account of the Holy Spirit could deal with a person such as Jonah in the ways that the biblical story portrays. I do not see how one could make it clearer than the texts cited above do that, on Aquinas's view, God is personally present to a person of faith in maximally responsive ways,

---

64   For an excellent discussion of this subject in connection with Aquinas's ethics, see Andrew Pinsent, *The Second-Person Perspective in Aquinas's Ethics: Virtues and Gifts* (London and New York: Routledge, 2012), especially chapter 4, in which Pinsent likens the fruition of second-person relatedness, an 'abiding in' the other, to a state of resonance.

communicating, counseling, and comforting, able to share rejoicing, as one friend does with another.

But, equally, I do not see how anyone could suppose that Aquinas is guilty of so great an inconsistency as to maintain this view of God when discussing the nature and actions of the Holy Spirit and yet also to hold that God is immutable, eternal, and simple, if by these attributes Aquinas means what some contemporary philosophers and theologians, friendly or unfriendly to classical theism, suppose Aquinas to mean. If God is not an entity (an *id quod est*) but only *being* (*esse*) alone, unable to act as a concrete particular does, incomprehensible to human beings, and by nature unable to respond to them, then Aquinas's views of the indwelling Holy Spirit, with the gifts and fruits of the Holy Spirit, are so inconsistent with his views of God as to be obviously ridiculous.

And there really are not two Aquinas's, one who wrote the questions on the divine attributes in the Prima Pars of the *Summa*, and one who wrote biblical commentaries. The same mind composed both. As far as that goes, although it is generally taken just as an expression of an almost incredible humility, we might actually take seriously what Aquinas himself says in the prologue to his *Summa theologiae*: "In this work, our intention is to teach those things that pertain to the Christian religion in a way suitable for the education of beginners."

If this work is his introductory textbook, then what did he himself take to be his more advanced works? It is not unreasonable to suppose that he would have taken his biblical commentaries to fall into this category. From his point of view, the biblical texts are God's revelation to humankind and so contain a kind of wisdom not available to unaided human reason alone. Why would he not suppose that commentary on God's wisdom constitutes a more advanced teaching than what he himself categorizes as a textbook for beginners? And if that surmise is correct, as I think it is, then the *Summa* needs to be read in light of the biblical commentaries.

In my view, the solution to the conundrum posed by seeing that Aquinas accepts both classical theism and these views of the Holy Spirit consists in recognizing that the interpretation of classical theism on the part of some contemporary philosophers and theologians is not the interpretation Aquinas himself held. For Aquinas, classical theism's view of God as immutable, eternal, and simple is not inconsistent with the view of God Aquinas presents in his discussions of the Holy Spirit's characteristics and relations with human beings.

The doctrine of eternity and the biblical God of Aquinas

To begin to see the consistency of Aquinas's position, it is helpful to start with the doctrine of eternity, as

Aquinas understands it.[65] Contrary to the way it is sometimes thought of, eternity is not just timelessness. Boethius, who gives the classical definition of eternity, says that eternity is "the complete possession all at once of illimitable life".[66] In SCG I c.15, echoing Boethius's definition, Aquinas describes God's eternity this way, "God is entirely without motion.... Therefore, he is not measured by time... nor can any succession be found in his being... [Rather,] his being [is] all at once (*totum simul*), in which the formula of eternity consists....".

In ST I q.10 a.1, Aquinas cites the combination of illimitability and the lack of succession as the heart of the concept of eternity. As he explains there, "Two things make eternity known: first, the fact that what is in eternity is interminable, that is, lacking beginning and end (since 'term' refers to both); second, the fact that eternity lacks succession, since it exists all at once."

In ST I q.10 a.2, Aquinas argues that God is his own duration; and in ST I q.10 a.2 ad 2, he explains that God endures beyond all ages (*durat ultra quod-*

---

65   To avoid clumsy locutions, I will leave this qualifier out in the subsequent discussion, but it should be understood throughout.

66   The translation of Boethius's definition is one Norman Kretzmann and I constructed; see my "Eternity" (with Norman Kretzmann), *Journal of Philosophy* 78 (1981), p. 429-458.

cumque saeculum).[67] These passages, combined with
the preceding texts, make it clear that the interminability of God's existence is to be understood as the
interminability of unending duration of some sort,
rather than as the interminability of a point or instant.[68]

So it is evident from these texts and others as well
that the concept of eternity as Aquinas accepts it is
the concept of a life without succession but with in-

---

67   That Aquinas means to adopt the Boethian definition for eternity is apparent in other places as well. The
Boethian formula, explicitly attributed to Boethius, is
also the basis for Aquinas's discussion of eternity in
Compendium theologiae cc.5-8, where Aquinas highlights the combination of being always (*semper*) and
atemporality in the Boethian concept of eternity. And,
to take another example, in QDV q.12, the question on
prophecy, Aquinas cites the Boethian formula as part of
his explanation of the way in which God knows future
things. For further discussion of Aquinas's views on
eternity, see Stump 2003, Chapter 4.

68   Cf. also *ST* I q.39 a.8 obj.1 and corpus; *ST* I q.46 a.1
obj.8 and ad 8. In *ST* I q.10 a.4, the first objection takes
as a premiss the claim that eternity, like time, is a measure of duration; in the reply to the objection, Aquinas
disputes only the assumption that time and eternity are
the same kind of measure of duration, not that eternity
is a measure of duration. In *ST* I q.10 a.4 ad 3, this
point is developed. In that reply, Aquinas maintains that
time as a measure of duration is the measure of motion,
whereas eternity as a measure of duration is the measure
of permanent being.

finite atemporal persistence or atemporal duration, where 'duration' is understood analogically with temporal duration. God's life consists in the duration of a present that is not limited by either future or past.[69] Nonetheless, nothing in the concept of eternity denies the reality of time or implies that temporal duration or temporal events are illusory.[70]

An analogy may help here. So consider Erwin Abbott's famous *Flatland*, a story about a two-dimensional world occupied by sentient two-dimensional creatures. In *Flatland*, one of these two-dimensional creatures, a sentient square, comes into conversation with a sentient sphere, who is an inhabitant of a three-dimensional world. The sphere has a terrible time explaining his three-dimensional world to his new friend, the two-dimensional square. As *Flatland* presents things, there is more than one mode of spatial existence for sentient beings. There is both the Flatland two-dimensional mode of spatial existence and the three-dimensional mode of spatial existence.

---

69   For more detailed discussion of this doctrine, see my "The Openness of God: Eternity and Free Will," in *New Essays Against Open Theism*, ed. Benjamin H. Arbour and Kevin Timpe (New York: Routledge, 2016).

70   For more discussion of these and related issues, see my and Norman Kretzmann's "Eternity," *Journal of Philosophy* 78 (1981), p. 429-458; "Prophecy, Past Truth, and Eternity," in James Tomberlin (ed.), *Philosophical Perspectives*, 5 (1991), p. 395-424; and "Eternity, Awareness, and Action," *Faith and Philosophy*, 9 (1992), p. 463-482.

That the sentient sphere is in three-dimensional space does not mean that the sentient square of Flatland is really somehow three-dimensional or that the square's mode of spatial existence somehow really has any of the three-dimensional characteristics of the sphere's mode of existence. In the story, the two spatial modes of existence, that of Flatland and that of the sphere, are both real; and neither is reducible to the other or to any third thing.

Boethius, Aquinas, and others who accept the doctrine of eternity suppose that an analogous point holds as regards temporal and eternal modes of duration. From their point of view, reality includes both time and eternity as two distinct modes of duration, neither of which is reducible to the other or to any third thing. Nonetheless, on their view, it is possible for inhabitants of the differing modes of duration to interact.

To understand the nature of the interaction, it is important to see the implications of the Boethian definition of eternity.

Consider first the matter of succession. Temporal events are ordered in terms of the A-series—past, present, and future—and the B-series—earlier than, simultaneous with, later than. Because an eternal God cannot be characterized by succession, nothing in God's life can be ordered in either of those series. Moreover, no temporal entity or event can be past or future with respect to, or earlier or later than, the whole life of an eternal God, because otherwise God would himself be part of a temporal series, and so there would be succession in God's life, as there cannot be on the Boethian definition of eternity.

On the other hand, eternity is also characterized by the duration of a present that is not limited by either future or past. Because the mode of existence of an eternal God is characterized by a limitless and atemporal kind of presentness, the relation between an eternal God and anything in time has to be one of simultaneity.

Of course, the presentness and simultaneity associated with an eternal God cannot be temporal presentness or temporal simultaneity. Taking the concept of eternity seriously involves recognizing that it introduces technical senses for several familiar words, including 'now', 'present', and 'simultaneous with', as well as for the present-tense forms of many verbs. The relations between eternity and time therefore require a special sense of 'simultaneity'.

In earlier work, Norman Kretzmann and I called this special sort of simultaneity 'ET-simultaneity', for 'simultaneity between what is eternal and what is temporal'. A relationship that can be recognized as a kind of simultaneity will of course be symmetric. But since its relata have relevantly distinct modes of existence, ET-simultaneity will be neither reflexive nor transitive. In particular, each of two temporal events can be ET-simultaneous with one and the same eternal event without being ET-simultaneous with each other.

If Flatland were finite and linearly ordered with an absolute middle, there might be an absolute Flatland *here*, which in the Flatland world could be occupied by only one Flatlander at a time. Nonetheless, if Flatland were small enough, then from the point of view of a human observer in the three-dimensional world, all of Flatland could be *here* at once. And yet it would not follow and it would not be true that all of Flatland would be *here* with respect to any occupant of Flatland. So it could be the case both that only one thing in Flatland could be *here* at once (with respect to the occupants of Flatland) and also that all of Flatland could be *here* at once (with respect to the inhabitants of the three-dimensional world). The reason for this apparently paradoxical claim is that all of Flatland can be encompassed within the metaphysically bigger *here* of the three-dimensional world.

An analogous point holds with regard to the present, on the doctrine of eternity. With respect to God in the eternal present, all of time is encompassed within the eternal present, insofar as all of time is ET-simultaneous with the eternal present. Just as the whole Flatland world can be *here* for someone in three-dimensional space, so all of time can be *now* for God in the eternal *now*. The logic of the doctrine of eternity has the result that every moment of time, as that moment is *now* in time, is ET-simultaneous with the whole eternal life of God. Or, to put the same point the other way around, the whole of eternity is ET-simultaneous with each temporal event as that event is actually occurring in the temporal *now*. But it does not follow and is not true that all of time is present with respect to anything temporal at any particular temporal location. Two separate points in Flatland could each be *here* with regard to an inhabitant of a three-dimensional world, without its being the case that these points are both *here* to each other in the two-dimensional world of Flatland. And the analogous point holds as regards time and eternity.

It may help to make the relations between eternity and time clear if we briefly consider the question: "Does an eternal God know what time it is now?"[71] For the sake of discussion, suppose that the indexical 'now' is ineliminable and that there is an absolute temporal present, as distinct from a present that is merely relative to some particular temporal entity. Could an eternal God know what time it is *now*, on this supposition?

On the supposition that there is an absolute present, then in time there is a fact of the matter about how far history has unrolled, so to speak. With regard to the inhabitants of time, at any given moment in time as that moment in time becomes present, history has unrolled *that* far. And this is something an eternal God can know. Furthermore, because the whole of eternity is ET-simultaneous with each temporal event as it is actually happening, an eternal

---

71   For more discussion of this question, see Stump 2003, Chapter 4.

God can know all the events actually occurring at any particular time as well as the temporal location of that time and its being experienced as absolutely present by temporal entities at that time.

But after these things, there is nothing further for God to know about what time it is now.[72] There is no time in the eternal now; and, from the standpoint of the eternal present, every temporal event, as it is part of the absolute temporal present, is present at once to the whole life of eternal God. In the life of an eternal God, no *temporal* moment has any more claim than any other to be *for God* the absolute present.

Just as in the example of Flatland and the three-dimensional world, once eternity is introduced, there are two different but equally real modes of duration; and *presentness* becomes relational. In relation to the unrolling of history, a moment of time may not yet be present. But in relation to the enduring and encompassing present of eternity, that same moment

---

72   For an opposing view, see Lynne Rudder Baker, "Eternal God —Temporal World," St. Thomas Lecture, KU Leuven, Belgium, March, 2016 (forthcoming). Considerations of space prevent my discussing Baker's paper in detail, but in my view an appropriate response to her concerns would highlight the way in which the metaphysically greater mode of duration of eternity allows God access to every moment of time as that moment is present in time. My drawing attention to the analogy with space in Abbott's *Flatland* is an attempt to give some aid to intuition on this score.

in time may be present to God, insofar as one and the same eternal present is ET-simultaneous with it.

Given the doctrine of eternity, then, God does not have foreknowledge. God knows any given thing or state of affairs that is a future contingent with respect to us only as it itself is temporally present, and not as it is future. Consequently, on the doctrine of eternity, there is no problem of *foreknowledge* and free will, since God's knowledge is ET-simultaneous with those events which are in the future with respect to us; God's knowledge is not located in time before the events that God knows. Analogously, and for the same reasons, God cannot change the past or act on the future. Such actions require a temporal location, without which there can be neither past nor future. Nonetheless, the proponents of the doctrine of eternity thought that, in the eternal present, God can directly know and affect events that are past or future with respect to us in time. For example, God can will in the eternal present that something occur or that something come into existence at any particular point in time, including those points that are past or future with respect to us.

Furthermore, if an eternal God is also omnipotent, as, of course, on classical theism he is, then God can do anything it is not logically impossible for him to do. In that case, even though God's actions cannot be located in time, God can bring about effects in time unless doing so is logically impossible for him. So the effects of God's actions can be in time even though God's action itself is not in time but in eternity. Aquinas himself is clear about this distinction. For example, in discussing creation in SCG, he argues that the creation of things in time does not imply succession on the part of the creator.[73]

There are, however, some actions that seem to require that the action have an existence and location in time. So, for example, an answer to a prayer apparently needs to be given *after* the prayer. Consequently, someone might suppose that an eternal God cannot answer prayer. But in fact this supposition is mistaken. An answer to prayer needs to be given *because of* the prayer; it is this counterfactual condition that is essential to the action of answering prayer, not any temporal relation between the answer and the prayer. And this counterfactual condition is one that an eternal God can meet. In one and the same eternal present, God can hear a prayer made at t_1 and also will because of that prayer at t_1 a temporal effect at t_2 that is an answer to that prayer. God's action will then count as answering prayer even though God's action is ET-simultaneous with both the prayer and the temporal effect caused by God's answer to the prayer.

Finally, some philosophers suppose that the doctrine of eternity rules out God's interacting with things in time for yet a different reason. So, for example, William Hasker says,[74] "I ... regard the doc-

---

73   SCG II.19.

74   Hasker 2004, p. 100.

trine of timelessness as coherent and intelligible....
But divine timelessness... does not help... in enabling us to understand God's actions in providence and prophecy."[75]

According to Hasker, it is impossible that God should use a knowledge "derived from the actual occurrence of future events to determine his own prior actions in the providential governance of the world."[76] Even if God's timeless knowledge of the future is not incompatible with human free will, on Hasker's view, God cannot use that knowledge in interacting with human beings.

On Hasker's way of thinking about the matter, even if God's knowledge is not *before* the future events that God knows, that is, even if there is no temporal succession as between future events and God's knowledge, there is a logical order. An event's obtaining is logically prior to God's knowing it. Future events must be *there* in order for God to know them. And, in that case, Hasker's point seems to apply: since a future event must be *there* for God to know it, it seems that God cannot use his knowledge of that future event to act on it. And for that rea-

---

75   I will not discuss the issue of prophecy further here. For a detailed discussion of the doctrine of eternity and prophecy, see my and Norman Kretzmann's, "Prophecy, Past Truth, and Eternity," in James Tomberlin (ed.), *Philosophical Perspectives*, 5 (1991), p. 395-424.

76   Hasker 1989, p. 176.

son, God cannot act on a future event in light of his knowledge of it.

And so we have the conclusion Hasker wants, without attributing succession to an eternal God. Even if it is eternal, God's knowledge of things future with respect to us seems useless for any action of God's on future events.

But this conclusion is mistaken. The fact that an event 2 at t_2 is ET-simultaneous with God's eternal present does not mean that God gets to event 2 too late to act on it, as it were. It is an error to suppose that God is unable to exercise causal influence on event 2 on the grounds that, for God, event 2 is *there* and fixed with the necessity of present.

To see this point, consider that because God is ET-simultaneous with temporal events that are prior to any temporal event 2, God can exercise causal influence on those prior events. And if God does so, the consequence will be that event 2 is what it is at least in part because of what God in the eternal present wills to happen at times prior to t_2. And, of course, since God is ET-simultaneous with every moment of time as that moment is present, God can exercise causal influence in the same manner at any time. What happens at t_n happens at least in part because of the causal effects which God in the eternal present wills to happen at times earlier than t_n.[77] In this way, without being himself in time, in one and

___

77   For all times other than the first instant of time, of
course, if there is such an instant.

the same eternal present, God can will in such a way
that he exercises causal influence over the whole temporally ordered causal sequence of events in time.

Of course, Hasker's point was about God's knowledge of events in time. But the explanation of an
eternal God's *actions* in time can be applied also to
an eternal God's *knowledge* of things in time. In the
example above, it is true that there is a logical dependence between event 2 at t_2 and God's knowledge of
event 2. God knows event 2 because event 2 obtains,
and not the other way around.[78] But, in the eternal
present, which is ET-simultaneous with every instant of time, God wills to exercise causal influence
at times before t_2 in such a way that event 2 at t_2 happens at least in part because of what God wills to
happen at times prior to t_2. God's knowledge of event
2, then, depends on event 2 at t_2; but event 2 itself
depends on God's causal influence on events prior
to t_2. Since God's knowledge of event 2 includes also
knowledge of his own causal influence on things that
helped to bring about event 2 at t_2, God's knowledge
of event 2 does not preclude God's acting in time in
such a way as to influence event 2.

The flaw in Hasker's argument for the uselessness
of God's eternal knowledge is the supposition that
the logical dependence of God's knowledge on the
temporal events known obviates God's ability to use
his knowledge to shape his actions in time. On the
doctrine of eternity, the logical dependence of God's

_____

78   Cf. Stump and Kretzmann 1998.

knowledge of a temporal event at t_n on that event does not rule out the causal dependence of that event at t_n on God's acts with regard to times prior to t_n, and those divine acts are manifestly included in God's knowledge. What is there at a time t_n for God to know is a function of what God does and knows that he does with regard to things prior to t_n. And so, in this sense, temporal events are in fact dependent on God's knowledge. On the doctrine of eternity, it makes sense to say, as Aquinas does, "Those things that are future in themselves are present in the providence of God, as Sirach (23:30) says, 'Before they were created, all things were known to the Lord our God.'"[79]

Therefore, just as nothing about God's eternal knowledge of future events rules out human free will, so nothing about God's eternity and the nature of knowledge in general rules out God's using his knowledge of temporal events to shape his actions with regard to things in time.

More generally, then, nothing about eternity itself precludes God's being responsive to his creatures. God's eternality does not rule out God's having effects in time or God's responding to things that temporal human beings do.

There remains yet just the special question about the personal presence of an eternal God, which was raised by Hasker and Lewis. The story of Jonah shows God not just engaged remotely in acts of will

---

79 *Commentary on Romans,* Chapter 4, lecture 3.

about what bits of conversation with God Jonah will hear at one time or another. In the story of Jonah, God is personally present to Jonah, personally engaged with him. But this is what Hasker and Lewis think is not possible if there is so great a metaphysical divide between God and Jonah as the gap between time and eternity implies.

But here we should ask what personal presence is. Hasker and Lewis are right to suppose that any attempt to capture personal presence solely in terms of direct and unmediated cognitive and causal contact misses something in the sense of personal presence even as between human beings. As I have argued elsewhere,[80] if one person Paula who is blind falls over another person Jerome when he is unconscious in her path, she may cause him to be moved by falling over him; and she may know by touch that it is a human person she has fallen over. Paula will thus have direct and unmediated causal and cognitive connection with Jerome; but she is not present to Jerome, in any normal sense of personal presence, in consequence of falling over him while he is unconscious.

As I have argued elsewhere,[81] what has to be added to the condition of direct and unmediated causal and cognitive contact in order to characterize personal presence is something psychologists call 'shared attention.' This is a cognitive state hard

---

80   See Stump 2010, Chapter 6.

81   Stump 2010, Chapters 4 and 6.

to define precisely but very familiar to us. Mutual gaze is one means for mediating a primary kind of shared attention; but there are many other kinds as well. Mutual gaze yields a particularly powerful kind of shared attention, but it is also possible for shared attention to be mediated by means other than vision. Blind children are capable of shared attention with their primary caregivers through sound; and even a blind and deaf child is capable of shared attention mediated by touch. As far as that goes, no sensory modality is necessary for shared attention; mutual interior awareness is sufficient. It is possible for one person to be engaged in mutual awareness of shared attention with another person without seeing, hearing, smelling, touching, or tasting that other person. For example, if two people are engaged in an animated conversation with one another that they conduct by means of email, they are aware of each other and sharing attention with each other, even if neither has perception of the other.

For personal presence, then, not only does there have to be direct and unmediated causal and cognitive contact between persons, but they have to be available for shared attention with each other as well. Nothing about God's eternity, however, rules out the mutual awareness of shared attention between God and human beings. On the contrary, Aquinas clearly supposes that, in the indwelling Holy Spirit's relations to human beings, shared awareness is central to the relation.[82] He stresses the intimacy of the Holy Spirit to the person of faith, and he emphasizes the union that results from this intimacy and the joy it yields.

So, to add to the examples already given above, Aquinas says, speaking to people of faith, "you, who are moved by the Holy Spirit, will know him. .... Note how intimate his indwelling is; [it is] in the depths of your heart: 'I will put a new Spirit within them.' (Ezek.11:19)."[83]

And, in explaining the way in which the Holy Spirit interacts with the mind of a person of faith, Aquinas emphasizes the union of love between such a person and the Holy Spirit. He says, "The mind of a human being is not moved by the Holy Spirit unless in some way it is united to the Holy Spirit..."[84]

In commenting on the line in 1 John that speaks about God abiding in a person of faith, Aquinas says,

the ultimate perfection, by which a person is made perfect inwardly, is joy, which stems from the presence of what is loved. Whoever has the love of God, however, already has what he loves, as is said in 1 John 4:16:

---

82   For a detailed argument that Aquinas's account of the infused virtues and gifts can and should be interpreted in terms of shared awareness, see Pinsent 2012.

83   *Commentary on the Gospel of John*, Chapter 14, lecture 4, p. 74.

84   ST I-II q. 68 a.4 ad 3.

'whoever abides in the love of God abides in God, and God abides in him.' And joy wells up from this.[85]

So, on Aquinas's own understanding of God's eternity, it is entirely consistent with the most intimate personal presence of the Holy Spirit to a human person, a presence that unites a person of faith to God; and shared attention is part of anything that can be considered union. In order to argue that Aquinas is wrong in this view, one would have to show that even omnipotence is insufficient to produce shared attention for God with a human person, because something about such shared attention is logically impossible. Such an argument would be difficult to make, in my view.[86]

Consequently, even as regards the issue of presence between an eternal God and a temporal human person, the doctrine of eternity does not preclude the kind of relations God has with Jonah in the biblical story. An eternal God can have the kind of engaged and personally present conversation with human beings the Bible portrays God as having with Jonah. That is because, in one and the same eternal now, God is ET-simultaneous with every moment of Jonah's life. And in one and the same eternal now, God can will that he make one speech to Jonah which Jonah apprehends at time t_1 and another speech to

---

85   *Commentary on Galatians*, Chapter 5, lecture 6.

86   For more discussion and defense of this claim, see my and Norman Kretzmann's "Eternity, Awareness, and Action", *Faith and Philosophy*, 9 (1992), p. 463-482.

Jonah which Jonah apprehends at time t_2. God's one act of will in one and the same eternal now can be for effects in different temporal locations. Furthermore, it is entirely possible and compatible with the doctrine of eternity that the speech God wills to introduce into time at t_2 is a function of what God in the eternal now knows that Jonah says at some time prior to t_2. Finally, on Aquinas's views, in a conversation between an eternal, immutable God and a temporal person such as Jonah, shared attention is possible; and so real personal presence between God and that human person is possible as well.

In fact, one consequence of God's eternality is that God can be more personally present to Jonah than any human person contemporary with Jonah could be. As regards Jonah, any human contemporary of his can be present only one time slice after another. When Jonah is thirty years old, for example, neither his three-year old self nor his sixty-year old self are available to his contemporary. But eternal God is present at once to every time of Jonah's life. None of Jonah's life is ever absent or unavailable for God, and at once, in the eternal now, God is available for shared attention with Jonah at any time in Jonah's life.

The doctrine of immutability and the biblical God of Aquinas

Someone might object that even if God's eternality does not preclude God's responsiveness, God's immutability does; but this is a mistaken objection. It is true that since change requires time, nothing eternal and therefore outside of time can change. An eternal God is immutable. But it does not follow that the plans of an eternal and immutable God cannot be altered or that God cannot be responsive to human beings.

An eternal, immutable God is not changeable across times since he does not exist at any times. At each and every time ET-simultaneous with the one eternal *now*, God is one and the same. And so an eternal, immutable God cannot do anything *after* something happens in time. But such a God can certainly act *because of* something that happens in time. In one and the same eternal *now*, God can both will to introduce into time t_1 an announcement to the Ninevites of the destruction of their city within 40 days after t_1 and also will to introduce into time t_2 the retraction of the destruction of Ninevah because the people repented between t_1 and t_2. In making this one simultaneous complex act of will, the plan of God is changing, but God is not changing. God is responding to what the Ninevites do, but his responsiveness does not require any alteration on his part. In one and the same eternal act of will, without alteration, an eternal, immutable God can will to introduce different effects into different points in time because of what human beings do at other points in time.

So nothing about God's immutability precludes God's having a conversation with Jonah in which what God says to Jonah is a response to what Jonah has said to God. The union in love that Aquinas supposes the indwelling Holy Spirit produces in every person of faith is a personal, engaged, interactive relation that is compatible with God's immutability as well as God's eternality. To suppose otherwise is to confuse the immutability and eternality of God with their frozen, static, temporal, and metaphysically limited analogues. By contrast, as the preceding comments on God's personal presence make clear, on Aquinas's views of eternality, an immutable, eternal God is maximally responsive to his temporal creation.

The doctrine of simplicity and the biblical God of Aquinas

Some people, however, have supposed that the doctrine of simplicity rules out precisely any kind of responsiveness on God's part. As I explained above, on the view of such philosophers and theologians, the doctrine of simplicity implies that God is identical to *being* (*esse*) alone. On their view, God must be distinguished from a being or an object (an *id quod est*). Furthermore, on the doctrine of simplicity, for all things other than God, there is a real distinction between what they are and that they are, between their essence and their existence; but, for God, the essence that is God is not different from God's existence. Therefore, unlike all created entities, God is his own essence, which is the same as his own being.[87] Since *being* is just *being* and nothing else, God has no accidents. But, then, as some contemporary philosophers and theologians suppose, this claim seems to entail that the only things God can do are the things God does in fact do.[88] In that case it is hard to see how God could be responsive to human beings.

To see why some scholars have supposed that this conclusion follows from the doctrine of simplicity, consider that if God could do otherwise than he does, then some characteristics of God would be contingent, not necessary. But contingent features of God would be accidents in God, or so it seems. In medieval logic, an accident is just a characteristic that a thing can have or lack and still be what it is.[89] Since the doctrine of simplicity rules out accidents

---

87   *ST* I.3.3.

88   The question whether God could do what he does not do, or refrain from doing what he does, is a well-recognized problem in the tradition of rational theology. Aquinas, for instance, discusses it several times—e.g., *In Sent* I.43.1.1-2; *SCG* II.23, 26-27; *Quaestiones Disputatae de Potentia Dei (QDP)* 1.5; *ST* I.25.5. I discuss this question further later in this book. For detailed examination of different interpretations of Aquinas's views on this score, see, for example, W. Matthews Grant and Mark Spencer, "Activity, Identity, and God: A Tension in Aquinas and his Interpreters", *Studia Neoaristotelica*, forthcoming.

89   See, for example, *Peter of Spain (Petrus Hispanus Portugalensis)*, *Tractatus. Afterwards Called Summule logicales*, ed. L.M. de Rijk (Assen: Van Gorcum, 1972):

in God, it seems to follow that everything about God is essential to him and therefore necessary for him. For this reason, on the sort of interpretation of divine simplicity represented by Elders and others in the quotations given at the outset here, God must be the same in all possible worlds, as contemporary philosophers would put it. And so, on this way of thinking about simplicity, God would do what God in fact does no matter what human beings do. And if that is so, it is indeed very hard to see how God could be responsive to anything human beings do.

It is perfectly clear, however, that Aquinas does hold that God *can* do other than he does. In fact, Aquinas takes God to be possessed of choice or *liberum arbitrium*,[90] and he argues for this claim vigorously in a variety of places. But, for Aquinas, *liberum arbitrium* is the power for choosing among alternative possibilities. In addition to the standardly cited passage in ST I q.19 a.10, for example, Aquinas says in *Quaestiones Disputatae de Veritate* (QDV) q.24 a.3, "there remains to God a free judgment [*liberum iudicium*] for willing either this or that, as there is

---

"*Accidens est quod adest et abest praeter subiecti corruptionem*," (p.23).

90 The notion of *liberum arbitrium* is not equivalent to our notion of free will but is rather a narrower concept falling under the broader concept of freedom in the will. For more explanation of Aquinas's understanding of *liberum arbitrium*, see Stump 2003, Chapter 9.

also in us, and for this reason we must say that *libe-rum arbitrium* is found in God."

In particular, Aquinas holds that God was free to create or not to create. God's creating was not brought about in God by any necessity of nature.[91] And since this is so, with regard to creating, God could do other than he did. In fact, God did create; but it was open to God not to create. Not creating is therefore something that God could have done but did not do.

Thomists have typically supposed that Aquinas's claim that God has no accidents is consistent with Aquinas's claim that God could do other than he does. For example, Garrigou-Lagrange says, "God's free act of creation, although it would be possible for Him not to act, is not an accident."[92] And later he says, "God is absolutely immutable, although it was in His power not to choose that which He freely chooses from eternity. For this free choice is not even in the least degree a superadded accident in God, and it posits no new perfection in Him."[93]

But how are these positions to be reconciled if God is *being* (*esse*) alone? If God can do other than he does, then it is possible for God to exist as God and yet act differently from the way he actually does act. In that case, however, the way God actually acts

---

91   See, for example, SCG II.23.

92   Reginald Garrigou-Lagrange, *The One God* (St.Louis and London: Herder, 1943), p. 190-191.

93   Garrigou-Lagrange 1943, p. 511-512.

is not necessary to him. Hence, that God acts in the way he does is a contingent fact about God. For this reason, God's acting in this way certainly does appear to be an accident of God's. And yet Aquinas holds not only that God has no accidents but even that God is his own nature, which some scholars take to be *esse* alone. So, since the nature of *esse* is invariable, it seems that God cannot do other than he does. Consequently, God could not be responsive to human beings, as he is in the story of Jonah. It could not be the case that if Jonah had done otherwise, God would have done otherwise as well.

We can put the conundrum this way. Since no one whose will is entirely bound to just one set of acts makes real choices among alternative acts, it looks as if taking God to be only *esse* leads to the conclusion that God has no alternative to doing what he does. On the other hand, if we begin from the other direction, by taking it for granted that God does make choices among alternatives, then it seems that God cannot be only *esse*. And, in that case, on the view of some scholars, it would follow that God is not absolutely simple.

It is important to be clear at this point that Aquinas, who certainly takes the doctrine of God's simplicity as foundational to his philosophical theology, himself maintains explicitly and in detail, in multiple places, not only that God has free will and creates the world freely, but also that God can do otherwise than God does. And if it is possible for God to do other than he does, then it is possible for God to do something that God does not do in the actual world or to omit something that God does do in the actual world. And so God is not the same in all possible worlds. Consequently, it is possible for God to do what God does because of something that human beings do. It could be true even for a simple God that if Jonah had done otherwise, God would have done otherwise as well. And therefore, on Aquinas's own views, God can be responsive to human beings.

Those who suppose (contrary to Aquinas) that a simple God cannot do other than God does and those who, contrary to their own views, find themselves stuck with this conclusion go wrong because they interpret Aquinas as holding that God is *being* alone. In fact, Aquinas's position is more nuanced and more sophisticated.[94]

---

94   For helpful discussion of related metaphysical issues, see Michael Rea, "The Problem of Material Constitution," *The Philosophical Review* 104 (1995) 525-552; "Sameness Without Identity: An Aristotelian Solution to the Problem of Material Constitution," *Ratio* 11 (1998) 316-328; "Constitution and Kind Membership," *Philosophical Studies* 97 (2000) 169-193; "Relative Identity and the Doctrine of the Trinity," *Philosophia Christi* 5 (2003) 431–446; "Material Constitution and the Trinity," (with Jeff Brower), *Faith and Philosophy* 22 (2005) 487–505; and "Understanding the Trinity," (with Jeff Brower), *Logos* 8 (2005) 145–57. For a discussion of divine simplicity different from that presented here but helpful in this connection, see Jeffrey Brower, "Simplicity and Aseity," in *The Oxford Handbook to Philosophical Theology*, eds. Michael

To see his position, it is helpful to look carefully at his commentary on Boethius's treatise *De hebdomadibus*. In that commentary, Aquinas begins by making a careful distinction between *being* (*esse*) and a being or an entity (an *id quod est*).[95]

Among the many differences between *esse* and an *id quod est* that Aquinas highlights in this commentary, he calls attention to the fact that '*id quod est*' signifies something concrete whereas '*esse*' does not.[96] So, for example, he says,

> We signify one thing by '*esse*' and another thing by '*id quod est*', just as we signify one thing by 'running' ('*currere*') and another thing by 'a runner' ('*currens*'). For 'running' and '*esse*' signify in the abstract, just as 'whiteness' also does; but '*id quod est*', that is, 'an entity', and 'a runner', signify in the concrete, just as 'a white thing' also does.[97]

Rea and Thomas Flint (Oxford: Oxford University Press, forthcoming); "Making Sense of Divine Simplicity," *Faith and Philosophy* 25 (2008) 3-30; "A Theistic Argument Against Platonism (and in Support of Truthmakers and Divine Simplicity)," (with Michael Bergmann). *Oxford Studies in Metaphysics* 2 (2006) 357-386.

95   In this connection, cf. also *De ente et essentia*, c.3. Cf. also the entry on Being by John Wippel in *The Oxford Handbook of Aquinas*, ed. Brian Davies and Eleonore Stump (Oxford: Oxford University Press, 2011).

96   *In De hebd.*, II. 22. The translations from this work are my own.

97   *In De hebd.*, II. 22.

Aquinas also emphasizes the fact that an entity (an *id quod est*) is a particular[98] whereas *esse* is not. In these and other ways, Aquinas argues for the metaphysical difference between *esse* and *id quod est*. And he concludes that discussion this way:

> it is evident on the basis of what has been presented that in composite things *esse* and *id quod est* differ as regards the things themselves (*realiter*) .... And so [Boethius] says that in every composite thing, the *esse* [of a thing] is not the same as the composite thing [the thing as an *id quod est*].[99]

It is this kind of discussion that leads some scholars to the conclusion that God is only *being* itself. Since, on the doctrine of simplicity, God is *esse*, and *esse* is distinct from *id quod est* in the ways Aquinas outlines in this commentary (and elsewhere), then, as the quotations I gave at the outset of this book indicate, some scholars conclude that for Aquinas God is not a being or an individual or a concrete particular at all.

It is an advantage of their interpretation of Aquinas's view of divine simplicity that it explains why Aquinas would suppose God has no accidents. Nothing which is not an *id quod est* could have accidents. For example, *redness* is not an *id quod est*, and it has no intrinsic accidents. It is the wrong *sort* of thing, we might say, to have intrinsic accidents. If we think of intrinsic accidents as belonging somewhere

---

98   *In De hebd.*, II. 24.

99   *In De hebd.*, II. 32.

in the nine Aristotelian categories other than substance, then it is easy to see why nothing that is not an *id quod est* should be thought to have intrinsic accidents. *Redness* does not have a certain size or quantity, for example; it does not engage in action or receive the action of anything else—and so on. *Redness* is what it is—redness—and nothing else at all. And the same thing holds for *esse* or *being*. In addition, with regard to something that is not an *id quod est*, even existence cannot be attributed to it.[100] Because *redness* is not an *id quod est*, then it might be true that there *is redness*; but its being *redness* would be all there is to it. For Aquinas, who is not tempted to Platonism in this connection, *redness* is not the kind of thing that can exist. Consequently, we cannot separate *redness* into itself and its existence. The same thing is true of *esse*. Something that is *esse* alone does not have existence, then, and there is consequently no distinction between *esse* and the existence of *esse*. If there were, *esse* would become something concrete and particular, an *id quod est* rather than only *esse*.

This part of Aquinas's commentary also gives us one helpful way in which to parse what is often referred to as 'the real distinction'. In this connection, 'real' harks back to Aquinas's discussion of *esse* and *id quod est* in this commentary. There, following the lead of Boethius, Aquinas first talks about the difference *in concept or idea* between *being* (*esse*) itself and a being (an *id quod est*); and he shows that in

---

100   For all those other than Platonists, of course.

concept these are as different as an abstract universal
is from a concrete particular. But then Aquinas goes
on to ask about this same distinction *in reality*, and
not just in concept. In reality, Aquinas maintains,
for every composite thing there is exactly the same
distinction—thus a *real*, rather than just a notion-
al, distinction—between *esse* and an *id quod est*. In
reality, a composite thing is a being (an *id quod est*)
that has being (*esse*). Its being an entity is one thing;
its having being (*esse*) is another. And so, for every
composite thing, there is a real distinction between
what it is and that it is.

But in this same commentary Aquinas makes ex-
plicit that, on the doctrine of simplicity, in reality,
God is—somehow, in some way we do not understand—both *being* itself and also a being, both *esse*
and *id quod est*. So, for example, he says, "In simple
things, in reality (*realiter*), *esse* itself and *id quod est*
must be one and the same."[101]

After giving an argument that there cannot be
more than one thing which is both *esse* and also *id
quod est*, Aquinas sums up his position by saying
"This one sublime simple is God himself."[102] And
later in that same work, he says, "[in God] *esse* and
quod est do not differ."[103]

For Aquinas, then, on the doctrine of simplicity,
being (esse) and a being (an *id quod est*) are somehow

101   *In De hebd.*, II. 33.

102   *In De hebd.*, II. 35.

103   *In De hebd.*, V. 66.

the same in God. And for this reason, contrary to what some scholars have maintained about Aquinas's view, for Aquinas God is not just *being*, but rather *being* which somehow also subsists as a being or an *id quod est*. On Aquinas's view, it is right to say that God is *esse*, but this *esse* is somehow also an *id quod est*. That is, it is acceptable to say that God is *being*, provided that we understand that this claim does not rule out the claim that God is an entity, a concrete particular, an individual, an *id quod est*.

Consequently, on Aquinas's view, there is something false about conceiving of God as *esse* alone (or as *id quod est* alone). That is why Aquinas says,

> Those material creatures that are whole and subsistent are composite. But the form in them is not some complete subsisting thing. Rather, the form is that by means of which a thing *is*. For this reason, all the names imposed by us to signify some complete subsisting thing signify in the concrete, as is appropriate for composite things. But those names that are imposed to signify simple forms signify something not as subsisting but rather as that by means of which a thing is, as for example 'whiteness' signifies that by means of which something is white. Therefore because God is both simple and subsistent, we attribute to God both abstract names—to signify God's simplicity—and concrete names—to signify God's completeness and concreteness. Nonetheless, each kind of name falls short of God's mode [of being], just as our intellect does not know God as he is, in this life.[104]

---

104   *ST* I q.13 a.1 ad 2. Cf. also *SCG* I c.30.

In SCG, Aquinas puts the point even more strongly. He says, "For every simple thing, its *esse* and *id quod est* are one; for if they were different, then simplicity would be removed."[105]

In other words, taking God to be only *esse* or *being* alone is incompatible with taking God to be simple.

Those who take the doctrine of simplicity to imply that God is not an entity but is only *being* therefore misread Aquinas's position. In effect, their interpretation takes the doctrine of simplicity to make God metaphysically more limited than concrete things such as composite human beings, who can do otherwise than they do. But this is to get the doctrine upside down. The doctrine of simplicity implies that at the ultimate metaphysical foundation of all reality there is *esse*. But it also implies that this *esse*, without losing any of its characteristics as *esse*, is something subsistent and concrete, a particular, an individual (an *id quod est*) with more ability to act and with more freedom in its acts than any concrete composite entity has.

This interpretation of Aquinas's account of divine simplicity also serves to correct the misconstrual of Aquinas's prologue to ST I q.3. When Aquinas says of God that we do not know of God what he is (*quid est*), he is not espousing a radical *via negativa*, as some scholars have supposed. He is maintaining only that, on the doctrine of simplicity, what we do not know is the *quid est*, the quiddity, of God. As

---

105   Cf. also, e.g., SCG I.c.38.

Aquinas explains this point elsewhere, "With regard to what God himself is (*secundum rem*), God himself is neither universal nor particular."[106]

It is not that Aquinas fails to see that there is an incompatibility between *esse* and *id quod est*, or that he supposes the laws of logic do not hold in God's case. Rather, on his view, we do not know what kind of thing it is which can be appropriately characterized both as *being* itself and also as a being. In fact, God's true nature is unknown to us, at least in this life. Human reason can see that human reason cannot comprehend the *quid est* of God. But what human reason can comprehend is that, whatever God's nature really is, it is such that those things true of *esse* *and* those things true of an *id quod est* should both be affirmed of it, even if differently, and in different contexts.

Consequently, with regard to the quiddity of God, the best we can do is a kind of quantum metaphysics, analogous to the physics that characterizes light as both a wave and a particle. In some contexts, we can say appropriately that God is *esse*; and in other contexts, we can say appropriately that God is a being, just as in some contexts we can say appropriately that God is love and in other contexts we can say appropriately that God is loving. But neither claim rules out the other, on the doctrine of simplicity, as Aquinas interprets it. On the doctrine of simplicity, as Aquinas understands it, it is not strictly speaking

---

106 *ST* I q.13 a.9 ad 2.

correct to assert just that God is *esse* (or just that God is an *id quod est* either).

Furthermore, just as the human inability to understand fully the nature of light is compatible with a developed quantum physics, so the human inability to know the quiddity of God is compatible with a great deal of positive knowledge about God. Aquinas himself bluntly rejects the view that human beings can have no positive knowledge of God. In *Quaestiones Disputatae de Potentia Dei* (QDP) q.7 a.5, for example, he says,

> the understanding of a negation is always based on some affirmation. And this is clear from the fact that every negation is proved by an affirmation. For this reason, unless the human intellect knew something affirmatively about God, it would be unable to deny anything of God.

Since it is right to say that God is *esse*, even if God's real nature is not correctly and precisely specified as identical to *esse*, then it is also right to say that God has no accidents. Nothing characterizable as *esse* can have accidents, any more than *redness* can have accidents. *Redness* is redness and not redness plus accidents. *Redness* is only its own nature. The same points apply to God, as the doctrine of simplicity affirms. But one very big metaphysical difference between *redness* and God lies in the difference between the nature of *redness* and the nature of the subsistent *esse* that God is. *Redness* is not the kind of thing that exists, since it is not a particular. But the *esse* that is God is not a universal like *redness*. Rather, this *esse* is such that it is also right to say that it is an *id quod est*. As such, it is right to say that it is a particular, a being, an entity, and that it does exist. Since it nonetheless remains right to say of it that it is *esse*, it is right to say that there is nothing to it except its nature as *esse*. Even its existence, then, is its *esse*.

Similar things have to be said about God's acts. As Plantinga rightly claims, nothing that is only an abstract universal could act. But because it is also right to say that God is an *id quod est*, it is right to hold that God has the power to act and does act. Nonetheless, when God acts, it is also right to say that what acts is *esse*; and so God's acting remains within God's nature as *esse*. That is, the acts engaged in by the *esse* that is also an *id quod est* are not added on to *esse* as something additional to *esse*. In acting, the *esse* that is God remains *esse*; it does not become *esse* plus the property of acting. On this way of understanding divine simplicity, when the *esse* that is God acts, its action is not an accident in it. This is not because *esse* is an inert universal like *redness*, which is the same in all possible worlds. Rather, because this *esse* is subsistent, because it is also an *id quod est*, it is more active than anything composite is, and it has more power to do otherwise than any composite entity does.

On the doctrine of simplicity, then, the *esse* that is the ultimate foundation of reality has the power to do more than created, composite things can do but without its ceasing to be *esse*. In the power and the richness that is the subsistent *esse* which God is, God can do otherwise than he does without ceasing thereby to be *esse*. And that is why creation is a free and not a necessitated act on the part of a simple God.[107]

On this view, our mode of speaking is irreducibly inaccurate as regards God, but we can nonetheless see how to frame a quantum metaphysics, just as we can work out the mathematics of a quantum physics, even if our mode of speaking about light is analogously imprecise. The terms we use of God cannot be given any specific definition, let alone the same definition that those terms have when used of creatures. But Aquinas's account of analogical language for God is an attempt to explain and work around this imprecision in words describing God.[108] So, for example, Aquinas says,

---

107   For a discussion of this point and the relevant Thomistic texts, see Stump 2003, Chapter 3.

108   For a good, brief introduction, see James F. Ross, "Analogy as a Rule of Meaning for Religious Language," *International Philosophical Quarterly* 1 (1961), p. 468-502 (reprinted in A. Kenny, ed., *Aquinas: A Collection of Critical Essays* (Garden City, NY: Anchor Books— Doubleday & Co., 1969); for a more extended treatment, see James Ross, *Portraying Analogy* (Cambridge: Cambridge University Press, 1981).

no name is predicated univocally of God and creatures; but neither is it said purely equivocally, as some have said, because, on that view, nothing could be known or demonstrated of God. Rather, it would always fall into the fallacy of equivocation. ... we must consequently say that such names are said of God and creatures according to analogy....[109]

And so Aquinas denies that human beings cannot develop an intelligible account of God's nature or mode of existence. To suppose that we cannot know anything about God because we cannot apply predicates univocally to God and to creatures, Aquinas says,

is as much contrary to philosophers, who have demonstratively proved many things about God, as it is contrary to the Apostle, who says that the invisible things of God are clearly seen, being understood by means of those things which are made (Romans 1:20).[110]

Finally, there is the issue of passivity. As the quotations from Garrigou-Lagrange given above show, some scholars suppose that if God wills what he does because of something human beings do, then there is passivity in God.

Now, as I have been at pains to show, Aquinas himself thinks that a God who is pure act can nonetheless do other than he does, and the ability to do other than one does is sufficient for responsiveness. Therefore, God does not need to have any potenti-

---

109   *ST* I.13.5.

110   *ST* I.13.5.

ality in order to be responsive. So we can put to one side the concern that there has to be potentiality in a responsive God. But, as the passage from Garrigou-Lagrange highlights, there is an additional worry here, and it is also derived from simplicity. Since God cannot have accidents, it seems that nothing can have a causal effect on God, and so nothing can act on God either. Consequently, God cannot be passive. Is this conclusion by itself enough to rule out God's responsiveness to creatures?

Here it is important to be clear about what Aquinas himself takes passivity to be. In a representative explanation of passivity in the course of a discussion of God's power, Aquinas says, "a thing is passive (*patitur*) to the extent to which it is in potentiality;"[111] and by way of clarification he says, "Passive power is the principle of being acted on by another (*principium patiendi ab alio*)...."[112]

The question, then, is whether if God wills what he wills or knows what he knows because of something a creature does, there is passivity in God in this sense Aquinas has in mind.

The first thing to see here is that even a human being can will to do something because of what someone or something else does, without being acted upon by that other person or thing. So, for example, in writing this book I will to use the story of Jonah *because* of what the writer of the book of Jonah

---

111   *ST* I.25.1 ad 1.

112   *ST* I.25.1; cf. also *QDP* 1.1.

wrote; and so I am responsive to that writer and that writer's narrative. But that writer is not acting on me when I will in this way. That writer is dead as I will what to write.

Secondly, on Aquinas's views, even a human intellect need not be acted upon when it knows something because that something is the case. For Aquinas, the human intellect is always active when it knows. That is, in the process of cognition the human intellect acts on the phantasms derived from sensory input to abstract the intelligible species enabling intellectual cognition; the phantasms do *not* act on the intellect.[113] For Aquinas, there is in human beings an *active* or *agent* intellect.

So a human being can will or know something because of what something or someone else does without being acted upon. But then, in Aquinas's understanding of passivity as being acted upon, neither a human will nor a human intellect is passive in virtue of knowing what someone else does or in virtue of acting responsively to it.

A fortiori, neither God's will nor God's intellect is acted upon when God wills or knows something because of what creatures do. God's will is not efficiently caused to be in the state it is in when God freely wills to answer Jonah's prayer because Jonah prays it. God can therefore will what he does because of Jonah's prayer without its being the case

---

113   For Aquinas's views of the mechanisms of cognition, see Stump 2003, Chapter 8.

that God's will is acted upon by something outside himself. The will of a responsive God therefore need not be passive in order to be responsive. Similarly, God's intellect is not passive when God knows what Jonah does because Jonah does it, since God's intellect is active in the process of cognition just as much or more than human intellects are.

For these reasons, then, while the doctrine of simplicity on Aquinas's interpretation of it requires that there be no passivity in God, the claim that there is no passivity in God does not entail that God cannot be responsive either in knowing what creatures do or in willing something in response.

The doctrine of simplicity is the most fundamental and therefore also the most difficult of the standard divine attributes, and it is clear that many of the details of this interpretation of the doctrine of simplicity would benefit from further discussion in order to ward off the objection that the doctrine is just incoherent if it is interpreted in this way. But the important thing to notice is that this *is* the interpretation of divine simplicity that Aquinas, the exemplary proponent of classical theism, gives. And if we understand divine simplicity in the way Aquinas explicitly does, as perfectly compatible with the claim that God can do other than God does, then nothing about simplicity rules out God's responsiveness to human beings.

Consequently, it could be true even of a simple God that if Jonah had not prayed to God, then God would not have saved Jonah from the sea. In that case, there is a possible world in which Jonah does not pray and in which God does otherwise than God does in the actual world (the actual world of the story, that is) and does not rescue Jonah. Since the doctrine of simplicity does not rule out such claims, then it also does not rule out saying that God rescues Jonah *because of* Jonah's prayers. Consequently, we have what we need for the compatibility of divine simplicity with divine responsiveness to human beings. And there is also no problem in supposing that a simple God interacts with human beings as friends do with one another, with the mutual knowledge and mutual closeness that produces joy in the beloved, as Aquinas supposes the Holy Spirit does.

The implications

Someone might suppose that even if classical theism could be made consistent with the biblical portrayals of God, the complexity of the divine attributes central to classical theism is a theological burden. On this view, classical theism ought to be rejected not because it is inconsistent with biblical theism but because it is not necessary to biblical theism, which can be gotten without the complications of classical theism. For some philosophers, open theism is a manifestation of this sort of attitude.

In my view, this position is wrong-headed. Classical theism provides a powerful intellectual basis for the portrayal of God in the Bible, and any attempt to do without it will quickly run into complexities of its own that are either insoluble or insoluble without further intellectual apparatus that produces serious problems in its own right.

The issue of foreknowledge and free will is a case in point. As I have argued in detail elsewhere, the doctrine of eternity does solve this issue satisfactorily and also explains the way in which God's knowledge of future contingents can guide God's providence.[114] In my view, attempts to do the same jobs without the doctrine of eternity are not successful. If God is temporal and knows future contingents through temporal foreknowledge, then even with all the controversial metaphysics that this approach needs, it does not seem to leave room for the kind of

---

114   Most recently in "The Openness of God: Eternity and Free Will," in *New Essays Against Open Theism*, ed. Benjamin H. Arbour and Kevin Timpe (New York: Routledge, 2016). See also Stump 2003, Chapter 4; "Atemporal Duration: A Reply to Fitzgerald" (with Norman Kretzmann), *Journal of Philosophy* 84 (1987), p. 214-219; "Prophecy, Past Truth, and Eternity" (with Norman Kretzmann), in James Tomberlin (ed.), *Philosophical Perspectives*, 5 (1991), p. 395-424; "Eternity, Awareness, and Action" (with Norman Kretzmann), *Faith and Philosophy* 9 (1992), p. 463-482; "God's Knowledge and Its Causal Efficacy" (with Norman Kretzmann), in *The Rationality of Belief and the Plurality of Faith*, Thomas Senor (ed.) (Ithaca, NY: Cornell University Press, 1995), p. 94-124; and "Eternity and God's Knowledge: A Reply to Shanley" (with Norman Kretzmann), *American Catholic Philosophical Quarterly* 72 (1998), p. 439-445.

libertarian free will Jonah shows in his defiance of God in the story. And open theism's denial of divine foreknowledge of future contingents seems to me to yield an unsatisfactory account of divine providence. If in the story God does not have knowledge of Jonah's freely willed actions at every point in time, then it is hard to see how God could engage with Jonah and the Ninevites in the providential way God does in the story. So, in my view, neither the postulation of temporal foreknowledge nor the adoption of open theism can resolve the philosophical puzzles or stay true to the theological data in the way that the doctrine of eternity can.

And this is only the beginning. The doctrine of divine eternity also yields helpful results as regards the issue of praying for the past, the alleged incompatibility of immutability and omniscience, and other issues as well.[115] The most important of these issues has to do with the much misunderstood divine attribute of impassibility. Divine impassibility is often understood as the lamentable claim that God has no emotions and cannot suffer with human beings in their afflictions, or is even blissfully indifferent to human suffering.

Now it is true that in his divine nature God cannot have any *passions*, although a *passio* is not identical to an emotion, on most contemporary understandings of emotion. But God has a human nature as well as a divine nature, on traditional Christian views (which

---

115   For a discussion of these, see Stump 2003, Chapter 4.

Aquinas, of course, also accepts). On the Chalcedonian formula for the incarnate Christ, which is also part of Aquinas's classical theism, Christ is one person—who is the second person of the Trinity and is thus God—with two natures, one fully divine and one fully human.[116] On this understanding of the doctrine, it is true to say that God suffers and that God dies. In his divine nature, God neither suffers nor dies, since neither suffering nor dying is compatible with the divine nature; but God does suffer and die in the human nature God has assumed. In fact, on this understanding of the doctrine of the incarnation, at least one major point of God's assuming a human nature was God's making it possible for God to suffer and die. Therefore, on the Chalcedonian formula, God can both suffer and die, in the human nature God assumed.

But, for my purposes here, what is important to see is the difference made by the doctrine of eternity in this connection. If God is eternal, then God's having an assumed human nature is not something characteristic of God at some times but not at others. It is something characteristic of God always. On this view, God is never in the state of not having an assumed human nature. For this reason, on the understanding of God as eternal, God is never unable

---

116 I have examined the doctrine of the Incarnation and defended it against at least some of the major arguments attempting to show its incoherence in Stump 2003, Chapter 14.

to suffer or die. The capacity for suffering and dying is something characteristic of God always, in the human nature whose assumption is always with God. Consequently, on the doctrine of eternity, however we are to understand the doctrine of divine impassibility, it is not only true that God is able to suffer but it is also true that God knows a great many human emotions and human afflictions from his own experience of them. In God's eternal present, these emotions and that experience of affliction is never absent from God. The person who wept over Lazarus was God—God in his human nature but still God. And the grief that gave vent to those tears is also always present to God. If it were not so, there would be succession in God; and then God would be temporal, not eternal.

And so the doctrine of eternity has powerful and useful theological implications. Mutatis mutandis, analogous things can be said about the doctrine of simplicity.

As I have argued elsewhere, the doctrine of simplicity provides a solution for some otherwise apparently irresoluble perplexities, such as the apparent incompatibility of divine goodness and omnipotence and the apparent tension between divine goodness and divine free will.[117] Perhaps more importantly, it provides a metaphysical grounding for an objective ethics because it can ground morality in God's nature, as distinct from God's will. *Being* is correlative

---

117   See Stump 2003, Chapter 4.

with goodness. Since it is true to say that God is *being* (even if it is also true to say that God is an entity, an *id quod est*), then it is also true to say that God is goodness. What is good is therefore what is in accord with God's nature, and so it cannot vary with God's will any more than God's nature can. For the same or similar reasons, without presupposing anything dangerously close to a theological relativism, the doctrine of simplicity can give a meta-ethical grounding to virtue ethics that gives a principled explanation why some things rather than others count as virtues.[118]

Furthermore, the doctrine of simplicity can supply an explanation of the necessity of God's existence, of the sort that is often found wanting in versions of the cosmological argument, for example.[119] The answer

118   For further discussion of this claim and defense of it, see Stump 2003, Chapter 2.

119   See, e.g., "On the Radical Origination of Things," trans. Leroy E. Loemker, in *Gottfried Wilhelm Leibniz, Philosophical Papers and Letters*, 2nd edn. (Dordrecht: D. Reidel, 1969), p. 486-491. For a contemporary analogue, see Richard Swinburne, *The Existence of God* (Oxford: Clarendon Press, 1979). Swinburne thinks that God is a more rational stopping-point for explanation than is the universe itself, because "there is a complexity, particularity, and finitude about the universe which cries out for explanation, which God does not have.... the supposition that there is a God is an extremely simple supposition"(p. 130). The trouble with Swinburne's thesis is that he rejects the notion of God as an entity whose existence is logically necessary, and so it is not clear why we should share his intuition that theism constitutes a

to the question 'Why does God exist?' is that God cannot not exist, and the reason God cannot not exist is that, on the doctrine of simplicity, God is *esse* and *esse* cannot not exist. Or to put the same point another way, since God's nature is not impossible, it exists in all possible worlds; but, on the doctrine of simplicity, God is his own nature, and so God exists in all possible worlds. The necessity of God's existence is thus not one more characteristic of God which needs an explanation of its own but is instead a logical consequence of God's simplicity. Given the doctrine of simplicity, then, it is reasonable to claim that God is an entity whose existence—whose necessary existence—is self-explanatory. The explanation of the existence of an entity that is simple is provided entirely by the nature of the entity. And that conclusion supplies the justification, lacking in some versions of the cosmological argument, for claiming that God is a simpler stopping-point for universal explanation than the universe itself is. If we assume that God does not exist, the answer to the question 'Why is there something rather than nothing?', or

more rational stopping-point for explanation than atheism does. Philosophers such as Leibniz and Clarke, who rest their versions of the cosmological argument on the principle of sufficient reason, do tend to hold that God is a necessary being. But the trouble with their position is that they seem unable to account for the necessity of God's existence even though they appear to be obliged to do so by the very nature of the principle of sufficient reason that warrants their cosmological arguments.

the search for an explanation of all contingent facts, leaves at least one brute fact, at least one inexplicable contingent fact. But if God is simple, the causal chain of contingent facts has its ultimate explanation and ultimate source in a cause that is both necessary and self-explanatory. So the doctrine of simplicity, like the doctrine of eternity, brings with it considerable explanatory power.

On the other hand, when classical theism, understood as I have expounded it here, is combined with the portrayal of God given in the biblical stories or given in Aquinas's exposition of the indwelling Holy Spirit, then, I would like just to suggest, there are some implications worth further consideration too. For example, it is customary in philosophical theology to suppose that every created thing participates in being in virtue of being created by a God who is *being*. But if God is also irreducibly personal, an *id quod est* with one mind and one will, then every created thing somehow also participates in personhood in virtue of being created by such a God. This claim is not equivalent to some form of panpsychism, however.[120] Panpsychism attempts to find elements of

---

120   For excellent contemporary discussions of panpsychism, see Godehard Bruentrup's *Das Leib-Seele-Problem. Eine Einführung* (Stuttgart: 4. Aufl., 2012), esp. chapter 8; "Emergent Panpsychism," in *Panpsychism: Contemporary Perspectives*, ed. Godehard Bruentrup and Ludwig Jaskolla (Munich: Munich School of Philosophy, forthcoming 2016), in the Philosophy of Mind Series (ed. David Chalmers) at Oxford University Press; "Panpsychism,"

personhood intrinsically in every thing that there is. But what the melding of classical theism and biblical theism yields is a God who is personally engaged, personally present and interactive with everything that God has made. The traces of personhood left in things in virtue of being created by God, then, need not (or, better, should not) be thought of as intrinsic characteristics in the things themselves. Rather, these traces emerge in interaction with the creator, who is ever present to his creation. On this way of thinking about the traces of personhood in created things, it makes sense for God to say 'you' to the sea, but it does not make sense for any human being to do so, as perhaps it might on some contemporary versions of panpsychism. The sea might have traces of personhood only in relation to the mind and will of its creator, and not in its own right. There might

in *New Catholic Encyclopedia Supplement 2012-13: Ethics and Philosophy*, ed. Robert L. Fastiggi (Detroit, Gale: 2013), p. 1119-1120; "Alter Wein in neuen Schläuchen. Die Renaissance des Panpsychismus in der gegenwärtigen Philosophie des Geistes," in *Ein Universum voller 'Geiststaub'? Der Panpsychismus in der aktuellen Geist-Gehirn-Debatte*, ed. Tobias Müller and Heinrich Watzka (Paderborn: Mentis Verlag, 2011), p. 23-59; "Panpsychism and Structural Realism," in *The Mental as Fundamental. New Perspectives on Panpsychism*, ed. Michael Blamauer (Frankfurt: Ontos Verlag, 2011), p. 15-35; "Natural Individuals and Intrinsic Properties," in *Unity and Time in Metaphysics*, ed. Ludger Honnefelder, Edmund Runggaldier, and Benedikt Schick (Berlin/New York: Walter de Gruyter, 2009), p. 237-252.

be a kind of analogue to quantum entanglement between two physical particles in the personal engagement between God and the sea that there cannot be between one creature and another.

In a similar vein of thought, it is worth remarking that the phrase commonly used to express the nature of union with God in heaven, 'the beatific vision', is at best misleading and at worst inaccurate. No doubt, there is no full and complete union between God and a human person unless that human person is able to see God, in a way that produces joy for the human person who is seeing God. But no union of love is as one-sided or inactive as vision is. Just as it is a mistake to think of the God of classical theism as frozen, remote, disengaged, and static *being* itself, so it is a mistake to think of union with such a God as individual, unilateral, isolated admiration of *being* itself. Any union is mutual, and it will be characterized by activity in mutual personal presence and mutual interpersonal responsiveness of the kind the biblical stories suppose happens even in this life with human beings still in their post-Fall state.

Conclusion

Genesis maintains that human beings are made in the image of God. But the relation *being an image of* requires some reciprocal relation of similarity. Something X is an image of something else Y only if X resembles Y in some way; but then Y must also resemble X in some way. The biblical commitment to seeing human beings as made in the image of God makes it reasonable that the biblical God so often seems so human. Anthropomorphism is wrong-headed only if it is stupid. Philosophically literate anthropomorphism is exactly what one would expect of any worldview which affirms that human beings are made in the image of God.

Classical theism has been widely interpreted as rejecting any kind of anthropomorphism and as making God totally other than anything in the created world. The God of this version of classical theism is so unlike human beings that it is false even to think of God as a being or a concrete particular. On this view, the divine attributes of immutability, eternity, and simplicity preclude God's being anything like the deity portrayed in the Bible. Many people have supposed that classical theism, so understood, is religiously pernicious; and it is not hard to see why. Think just of Augustine's widely quoted line to God: "You have made us for yourself, and our hearts are restless till they rest in you." It is hard to imagine feeling that one's heart is restless till it rests in *being* alone. For that matter, it is hard to imagine praying fervently to *being* alone about anything. Who could say 'you' to *being* alone? And however hard it may be to understand heaven on the biblical portrayal of it, on this interpretation of classical theism heaven becomes as incomprehensible as *being* itself is supposed to be. What would it be for a human person to be united with *being* itself? Even ordinary liturgy and rites seem undercut by this view of the deity. The liturgical line "The Lord be with you!" sounds a lot like "The Force be with you!" if God is not a being at all. And the idea that God's simplicity makes God entirely incomprehensible to human beings in this life has the result that a person of faith is committing his life to a *je ne sais quoi*, a conclusion that ought to be deeply troubling for such a person.

In the Christian tradition, Aquinas is universally recognized as one of the main proponents of classical theism; and certainly he is committed to the view that God is immutable, eternal, and simple. But, as his views on the indwelling Holy Spirit make clear, the God Aquinas takes himself to be describing and explaining is a God in whose image human beings are made. Aquinas's God is highly responsive to human beings and engaged with them in personal and interactive ways. He is a God who is a particular and personal friend to every person of faith. And he looks very like the biblical God. The approach to the knowledge of God and the presence of God that Aquinas evinces when he explains the Gospel claim that the Father is seen in the incarnate Christ is of a piece with his general views about the nature of God and God's relations to human beings. The God Aquinas describes in his biblical commentaries and in his texts about the indwelling Holy Spirit is very human.

Aquinas can accept this characterization of God even while maintaining classical theism, because there is nothing in the logic of the attributes of immutability, eternity, and simplicity, as Aquinas understands them, that rules out God's acting in time, responding to human beings, conversing with them, and altering his announced plans for them because of what they do. As Aquinas understands these divine attributes, the God of the story of Jonah, the God who is the indwelling Holy Spirit who brings love and joy, could also be truly immutable, truly eternal, and truly simple.

And so, for that exemplary and influential proponent of classical theism Thomas Aquinas, the God of the philosophers and the God of the Bible are the same God—not because the biblical God is after all a frozen and unresponsive deity, but because the God of classical theism is truly the engaged, responsive, intimately present God of the biblical stories, in whose image human beings are made. [121]

---

121   The lecture version of this book was given at a workshop on Classical Theism at the University of St. Thomas (St. Paul) in 2015, which was supported by the John Templeton Foundation. I am grateful to the organizer of that workshop Timothy Pawl and to the Templeton Foundation for including me in that workshop. It was also given at a conference on God's Perfection sponsored by the Herzl Institute in Jerusalem. I am grateful to Yoram Hazony for including me in that conference. This book is better because of the discussion of the lecture version of the book at both events. I also owe a debt of thanks to my research assistant Matthew Shea for help with the notes on this book.

The Aquinas Lectures
Published by the Marquette University Press
Milwaukee WI 53201-1881 USA
http://www.mu.edu/mupress/

1. *St. Thomas and the Life of Learning.* John F. McCormick, S.J. (1937) ISBN 0-87462-101-1

2. *St. Thomas and the Gentiles.* Mortimer J. Adler (1938) ISBN 0-87462-102-X

3. *St. Thomas and the Greeks.* Anton C. Pegis (1939) ISBN 0-87462-103-8

4. *The Nature and Functions of Authority.* Yves Simon (1940) ISBN 0-87462-104-6

5. *St. Thomas and Analogy.* Gerald B. Phelan (1941) ISBN 0-87462-105-4

6. *St. Thomas and the Problem of Evil.* Jacques Maritain (1942) ISBN 0-87462-106-2

7. *Humanism and Theology.* Werner Jaeger (1943) ISBN 0-87462-107-0

8. *The Nature and Origins of Scientism.* John Wellmuth (1944) ISBN 0-87462-108-9

9. *Cicero in the Courtroom of St. Thomas Aquinas.* E.K. Rand (1945) ISBN 0-87462-109-7

10. *St. Thomas and Epistemology.* Louis-Marie Regis, O.P. (1946) ISBN 0-87462-110-0

11. *St. Thomas and the Greek Moralists.* Vernon J. Bourke (1947) ISBN 0-87462-111-9

12. *History of Philosophy and Philosophical Education.* Étienne Gilson (1947) ISBN 0-87462-112-7

13. *The Natural Desire for God.* William R. O'Connor (1948) ISBN 0-87462-113-5

14. *St. Thomas and the World State.* Robert M. Hutchins (1949) ISBN 0-87462-114-3

15. *Method in Metaphysics.* Robert J. Henle, S.J. (1950) ISBN 0-87462-115-1

About the Aquinas Lecture Series

The Annual St. Thomas Aquinas Lecture Series began at Marquette University in the spring of 1937. Ideal for classroom use, library additions, or private collections, the Aquinas Lecture Series has received international acceptance by scholars, universities, and libraries. Hardbound in maroon cloth with gold stamped covers. Uniform style. Some reprints with soft covers. Complete set (ISBN 0-87462-150-X) receives a 40% discount. New standing orders receive a 30% discount. Regular reprinting keeps all volumes available. Ordering information (purchase orders, checks, and major credit cards accepted):

Marquette University Press
Phone: (800) 247-6553
or order online at: http://www.mu.edu/mupress/

Editorial Address:
Dr. Andrew Tallon, Director
Marquette University Press
P.O. Box 3141
Milwaukee WI 53201-3141
Tel: (414) 288-1564 FAX: (414) 288-7813
email: andrew.tallon@marquette.edu